Jesus Christ – True God and True Man

Other Works of Interest from St. Augustine's Press

Kenneth Baker, S.J., *Doctrinal Sermons on
the Catechism of the Catholic Church*

James V. Schall, S.J., *The Regensburg Lecture*

James V. Schall, S.J., *Modern Age*

James V. Schall, S.J., *The Classical Moment*

James V. Schall, S.J., *The Sum Total of Human Happiness*

James V. Schall, S.J., *Remembering Belloc*

Marc D. Guerra, ed., *Jesursalem, Athens, and Rome:
Essays in Honor of James V. Schall, S.J.*

Ernest Fortin, A.A., *Christianity and Philosophical Culture
in the Fifth Century*

Servais Pinckaers, O.P., *Morality: The Catholic View*

Richard Peddicord, O.P., *The Sacred Monster of Thomism:
An Introduction to the Life and Legacy of Garrigou-Lagrange, O.P.*

Josef Pieper and Heinz Raskop, *What Catholics Believe*

Peter Geach, *God and the Soul*

Gabriel Marcel, *Man against Mass Society*

Dietrich von Hildebrand, *The Heart*

Robert Hugh Benson, *Lord of the World*

Peter Kreeft, *The Philosophy of Jesus*

Peter Kreeft, *Jesus-Shock,*

Philippe Bénéton, *The Kingdom Sufferth Violence*

Rémi Brague, *On the God of the Christians*

Benedict Ashley, O.P., and John Deely, *How Science
Enriches Theology*

H.S. Gerdil, *The Anti-Emile:
Reflections on the Theory and Preactice of Education against the
Principles of Rousseau*

Jesus Christ –
True God and True Man
A Handbook on Christology for Non-Theologians

Kenneth Baker, S.J.

ST. AUGUSTINE'S PRESS
South Bend, Indiana

Manufactured in the United States of America

1 12 13 14 15 16   19 18 17 16 15 14 13

Library of Congress Cataloging in Publication Data
Baker, Kenneth, S.J.
Jesus Christ, true God and true man:
a handbook on christology for non-theologians /
Kenneth Baker.
p. cm.
Includes bibliographical references and index.
ISBN 978-1-58731-403-2 (pbk.: alk. paper)
1. Jesus Christ – Person and offices. I. Title.
BT203.B35 2013
232'.8 – dc23   2012039816

∞ The paper used in this publication meets the minimum requirements of the American National Standard for Information Sciences Permanence of Paper for Printed Materials, ANSI Z39.481984.

St. Augustine's Press
www.staugustine.net

Contents

Introduction

Jesus Christ, true God and true man, who was born of the Virgin Mary in Bethlehem about 2,000 years ago, is the most important person who every set foot on planet earth. He was the most important person in world history because he was and is God Almighty in human flesh. Catholic Christians worship him as their Creator and Redeemer, and as their eternal Judge who, when he comes again in glory with his angels at the end of the world, will decide their fate for all eternity either in the happiness of heaven or in the misery of hell. Jesus Christ is not someone who can be ignored as just another religious genius. He came into this world of suffering and death to save all mankind from the consequences of sin – the sin of Adam at the beginning of the human race and the personal sins of all of his children. He is the only one who could do that since, as God, all of his actions have infinite value and merit.

The teaching of the Church about who Jesus of Nazareth is and what he is concerns every man, woman, and child who ever lived on this earth. The main points of that teaching are contained in the *Nicene Creed* which Catholics recite at every Sunday Mass. St. Peter expressed this truth very clearly to the Jewish leaders in Jerusalem when he said to them: "There is salvation in no one else, for there is no other name under heaven given among men by which we must be saved" (Acts 4:12).

Man in his moral weakness and doomed to die sooner or later has an immortal soul that will live on after the death of the body. Whether that future life will be one of happiness or misery depends on whether or not one dies in the state of sanctifying grace as a friend of Christ. So each person's destiny is essentially linked to his relationship to Jesus Christ, the only Savior of the world. It is because of this truth that Jesus, before he ascended into heaven to sit at the right hand of the Father, commissioned his Apostles to go into the whole world and preach the Good News of salvation in Christ, assuring them that he would always be with them in spirit to assist and strengthen them (see Matt. 28:18–20).

Because Jesus Christ is the only source of salvation, it is crucial for each person to know Christ and to become a member of his Mystical Body or Church. It is a sad fact that many Catholics have only a vague idea of their religion; they do not know that Jesus is both God and man; they do not know that the Mass is an unbloody sacrifice and a re-presentation of the bloody death of Jesus on Calvary; they do not know that Jesus is truly present – body, blood soul and divinity – under the appearances of bread and wine after the consecration by the priest at Mass. In short, they do not know their basic catechism, which contains divine revelation and the teaching of the Church based on it about Jesus, his Church, and God's plan of salvation for mankind.

It is because of the extensive ignorance among Catholics about Jesus Christ that I decided to write this short handbook on Christology as a way of instructing serious Catholics about Jesus, the object of their religion. The word "Christology" means the science or study of Christ. This little book offers a brief summary of Catholic doctrine about Jesus Christ. Its purpose is to explain in clear language who Jesus is, why he came into this world, and why he is important for the happiness and eternal future of each human person.

Christology, as it has been developed by bishops and theologians for two millennia and formulated in technical language, can be very complicated and difficult to understand for the ordinary lay person or non-theologian. It has its own terminology which has developed over hundreds of years. In this book I have tried to explain the essential truths about Jesus Christ in clear language that all can understand. The book does not attempt to cover everything that can be said about Jesus, such as his birth, his childhood, and his hidden life of about thirty years. It does not deal with the Church he founded on Peter and the Apostles, nor does it deal with the seven sacraments which are the instruments of sanctification.

The book concentrates on the divine Person in Jesus, who subsists in two natures – the divine nature and the human nature. This is the Word of God and the Second Person of the Blessed Trinity in the flesh (John 1:14). It also deals with the question of why God became man in Jesus Christ, namely, to save man from sin and the sad consequences of sin, which are death and damnation.

For the last fifty years or so sermons and homilies in Catholic Churches have emphasized preaching on the Bible. That is well and good, but there is a large body of Catholic doctrine about the Holy Trinity, the Incarnation, grace, and the Last Things that has been only alluded to briefly or completely ignored. The purpose of this little volume is to fill the gaps of ignorance about the solemn doctrinal teaching of the Church about our Lord and Savior Jesus Christ.

The doctrine contained in this handbook is based on the *Catechism of the Catholic Church* and the teaching of St. Thomas Aquinas contained in the Third Part of his Summary of Catholic Theology (*Summa Theologiae* III, Questions 1 to 59). The text itself is a revision and expansion of the material contained in Volume II of my previous work entitled *Fundamentals of Catholicism* (Ignatius Press, San Francisco 1983), pp. 197–311.

Pope Benedict XVI recently published a two-volume work entitled, *Jesus of Nazareth*, which has been well received and has been read by millions of Catholics. Those volumes are not intended to be a historical life of Christ; rather, they contain profound meditations on the various events of his life and are based primarily on the Gospels of Matthew, Mark, Luke, and John. So it is mainly a scriptural presentation of the life of Christ rather than a doctrinal presentation. This little book can profitably be used as a companion to Benedict's *Jesus of Nazareth* because it spells out and explains the Church's doctrinal teaching about Jesus Christ that is alluded to but not explicitly covered by the Pope's work.

It is my hope that his handbook will help Catholics and others come to a better understanding of who Jesus Christ really is, both God and man, and why the Catholic Church proclaims that he is the only Savior of all mankind.

Kenneth Baker, S.J.
April, 2012

Chapter 1
Jesus of Nazareth Is True God

Jesus of Nazareth, who lived in the Near East (the present country of Israel) 2,000 years ago, is the most important person who ever walked on this earth. He is the most important person because he is God Almighty in visible form as a man of flesh and blood. Jesus is both man and God. In his visibility he is man, a descendant of King David and the Son of Mary of Nazareth. Invisibly he is the Second Person of the Blessed Trinity, who has assumed to himself a human nature but not a human person. A small spark of his divine glory shone through him at his Transfiguration on Mount Tabor. Jesus, therefore, is not a human person but a divine Person, the Word of God who is consubstantial with the Father. He and the Father are one. When the Apostle Philip asked him to show them the Father, Jesus said, "Have I been with you so long, and yet you do not know me, Philip? He who has seen me has seen the Father. . . . Do you not believe that I am in the Father and the Father in me?" (John 14:9–10).

Jesus of Nazareth is the only-begotten Son of the Father. He lived on this earth for about thirty-three years. In his last three years he preached a new covenant with God based on love rather than fear. He gathered disciples around himself and taught them new truths about God and man. He worked miracles by instantly curing dis-

5

eases and raising people from the dead. Because he was misunderstood by the religious leaders of Israel, he was persecuted and eventually put to death in agony on the cross. Three days later, by his own power as God, he rose from the dead and appeared to his disciples over a period of forty days. Then he ascended into heaven and was seated at the right hand of the Father. From his heavenly throne he sent the Holy Spirit on his Apostles in the Upper Room on Pentecost. In the power of that Spirit, they were emboldened to go forth into the whole world to preach the Good News of eternal salvation through faith in Jesus Christ. On that very day Peter preached the Good News about Jesus Christ to a large crowd in Jerusalem, and 3,000 people were converted to faith in Jesus Christ as the Savior of the world (see Acts 2).

Jesus is the fulfillment of all the prophecies of the Old Testament. Everything in the Old Testament points, in one way or another, to Jesus and the Church he founded. The New Testament is the fulfillment of the Old, but it is also totally new. The difference is that Jesus is not merely a prophet, like Isaiah or Jeremiah or John the Baptist. They were illuminated by the Spirit of God to proclaim his word, to rebuke sinners, and to lead the people back to the worship of the true God. The huge difference is that Jesus is not just a prophet who transmits the word of God to the chosen people; he is the Word of God in the flesh; he is the God of the Old Testament, the Lord who created heaven and earth, the Lord to whom Solomon's majestic Temple in Jerusalem was dedicated and who was present in some way in the holy Ark of the Covenant in the Holy of Holies. As such he proclaims himself as the object of faith and worship. He promises eternal salvation and eternal happiness to those who believe in him and put in practice his commandment to love God and to love one's neighbor. St. John stated it beautifully when he said: "For God so loved the world that he gave his only son, that whoever believes in him should not perish but have eternal life" (3:16).

By establishing himself as the object of worship Jesus created a new religion that is essentially different from the religion of the Old Testament. Jesus is not like the founders of other religions and philosophies. Moses, Buddha, Confucius, and the creators of Hinduism did not themselves claim to be God; they did not set themselves up as the objects of worship. As religious genuses, they strove to teach their followers how to find God in their lives. Jesus is not like that. He is God Almighty, hidden in the flesh of Jesus of Nazareth. Gradually he revealed to his disciples who he was. Even though they absorbed his doctrine and even though they saw all his miracles, like raising people from the dead and walking on water, they still did not understand that this Jesus of Nazareth is more than a prophet – that he is God in the flesh. Even after his resurrection from the dead, they did not understand that Jesus is God. They still thought of him as an earthly Messiah and asked him if he would make Israel a great nation again (Acts 1:6). But a week after the resurrection one of the Apostles, Thomas the Doubter, after seeing the risen Christ and touching his wounds, was given the gift of faith in Jesus as the Son of God and uttered those immortal words, "My Lord and my God!" (John 20:28).

Forty days after his resurrection Jesus ascended into heaven from the top of the Mount of Olives, about a mile east of Jerusalem. He told his Apostles that they would receive the gift of the Holy Spirit in nine days on the feast of Pentecost. When that happened they were enlightened mentally and now could see that Jesus was both God and man. Jesus had already given them the light to understand the Scriptures when he said that everything written about him by Moses, by the prophets, and by the Psalms had to be fulfilled: '"Then he opened their minds to understand the scriptures" (Luke 24:45). So after the Holy Spirit descended on them on Pentecost they were able to put it all together and to know with infallible certainty that Jesus is the promised Messiah, that he is truly God, and that he is the Savior of the world. With that knowledge and that conviction they set out to convert the world to Christ and to establish his Church everywhere. They were so convinced of the divinity of Jesus of Nazareth that they shed their blood in defense of their faith. The brothers Peter and Andrew were both crucified just like their Lord and Master.

Since Jesus is God and the Messiah or Christ, he is the Savior of the whole world. He was born, lived, suffered, died, resurrected, and ascended into heaven for all mankind, both Christian and non-Christian. This means that anyone who attains eternal salvation and happiness in heaven for all eternity achieves that through the help and grace of Jesus Christ, who is the only Savior of the world. St. Peter put it very well when he said to the rulers in Jerusalem, "There is salvation in no one else, for there is no other name under heaven given among men by which we must be saved" (Acts 4:12).

A key question in the four Gospels is: Who is Jesus of Nazareth? Is he a prophet? Is he the Messiah? The belief of the Church about precisely who Jesus is and what he did during his earthly life and how he how relates to us from his place in heaven at the right hand of the Father is crucial for our own Christian existence. If he is both God and man and if he came into this world of time and space in order to show us how to attain happiness in the next life after our earthly pilgrimage is over, then the success of my life depends on listening to him and doing what he says.

Those who listen to Jesus Christ and follow him are *Christians.* In order to understand properly what it means to be a Christian we must know clearly who Jesus is and what he expects of us. The most basic belief of the Catholic Church about Jesus Christ is that he is truly God and truly the Son of God. The Church's belief in the divinity of Jesus Christ and in his divine sonship is clearly expressed in all the creeds that have been worked out in the course of history. The one most familiar to us in the Nicene-Constantinople Creed of 381 A.D. which we pray each Sunday at Mass: "I believe in one Lord, Jesus Christ, the only Son of God, eternally begotten of the Father, God from God, Light from Light, true God from true God, begotten, not made, consubstantial with the Father." The famous Athanasian Creed of the fifth century puts it this way: "The true faith is: we believe and profess that our Lord Jesus Christ, the Son of God, is both God and man. As God he was begotten of the substance of the Father before time; as man he was born in time of the substance of his mother. He is perfect God; he is perfect man."[1] What the Church believes, therefore, is that Jesus Christ possesses the infinite divine nature with all

1   Denzinger-Schönmetzer, *Enchiridion Symbolorum* (Verlag Herder, Freiburg in Breisgau, Germany 1965), 76 (henceforth DS); Neuner-Dupuis, *The Christian Faith* (Alba House, New York 2001), 17 (henceforth TCF).

its perfections by virtue of his eternal generation from God the Father. Since Jesus is God and therefore is endowed with infinite power and wisdom, he had a serious reason and a definite purpose in humiliating himself to the extent of becoming a frail, mortal human being. It is often repeated in the New Testament that that purpose is to give glory to God the Father and to save man from his sins. He died for our sins so that we can be reconciled with the Father, so that we can become adopted children of God and heirs of eternal life. He did something that no mere human being can do: make satisfaction to God for the sins of mankind, beginning with the original sin of Adam and Eve, which closed the gates of heaven and made us enemies of God.

From the time of Jesus' earthly life up to the present moment there have always been those who opposed him and rejected his claim to be true God and the Son of God. Because of this claim, the Pharisees accused him of blasphemy and had him put to death. The early heretics refused to do full justice to either his divinity or his humanity. The most common attitude in modern times is to look upon Jesus as a mere man – a religious genius, but still only a man. Modern liberal and process theologians will refer to Jesus as the "Son of God," but they do not understand the phrase in any metaphysical or real sense. They give the expression a moral meaning in the sense that Jesus had a unique awareness of the fact that God is our Father. Some say that Christ is the Redeemer of the world, not because he is the natural Son of God, but because he communicated to us the unique knowledge of God which he experienced. This view is quite common among Protestant liberal theologians; it is also the view of some contemporary Catholic dissidents, though it is usually disguised under rather ambiguous terminology in order not to come in conflict with the Magisterium of the Church.

The Old Testament offers a few hints of the divinity and divine sonship of the Messiah, but the full meaning of the relevant passages was not grasped by anyone until after Pentecost. Texts often adduced in this regard are Psalm 2:7, "The Lord said to me: 'You are my son, today I have begotten you'"; and Isaiah 7:14 which calls him "Emmanuel" or "God is with us." There are many other passages from the Psalms and the prophets that hint at the divinity of the Messiah, but they are not clear statements, and they were not understood in the full sense of divinity by the Jews of the time. It was not until after the Resurrection and Pentecost that the early Church came to the full realization that Jesus is God himself, the Second Person of the Blessed Trinity.

The New Testament contains many passages – in the synoptic Gospels, in St. John, in St. Paul – that either affirm or at least point to the full divinity of Jesus Christ. Thus, at the beginning of Jesus' ministry he is baptized by John the Baptist in the Jordan River. At that moment a voice from heaven said, "This is my Beloved Son in whom I am well pleased" (Matt. 3:17). At the transfiguration of Jesus on Mount Tabor a voice came from the clouds and said the same thing (see Matt. 17:5; Mark 9:7; Luke 9:35). Peter, James, and John heard the voice; it was followed by the injunction, "Listen to him." The biblical expression "my Beloved Son" means the same thing as "only Son."

The testimony of the heavenly Father was understood at the time by John the Baptist and the disciples as an assertion of Jesus' messianic mission. Their minds were not ready for the idea that Jesus is one in being with the Father and therefore both God and man. In the early Church, however, under the influence of the Holy Spirit its true significance as an affirmation of Jesus' divine sonship was fully realized and finds its expression especially in the writings of St. John and in the letters of St. Paul.

The constant belief of the Church since the Holy Spirit descended on the disciples in the Upper Room on Pentecost has been that Jesus Christ is true God and true Son of God. If one were to remove belief in the divinity of Christ from the Christian Creed it would make the lives of Christians and the bloody deaths of the martyrs basically unintelligible. They died for Christ because they had hope of gaining eternal life in heaven through his intercession and his grace.

The divinity of Jesus in Matthew, Mark, and Luke

The Gospels of Matthew, Mark and Luke – called the *synoptic* Gospels because they give a similar and brief account of Jesus' life and death – present a Jesus who is aware of his unique relationship to God the Father. To anyone who has studied the Gospels or prayed with them for some time it is obvious that Jesus of Nazareth is no ordinary human being. There is something special, something different, something unique about him. That "something" is his consciousness of being the true, consubstantial Son of God.

We must remember, however, that the synoptic Gospels were written, most probably, between twenty and fifty years after the early preaching of the Apostles and after the first Christian communities had been functioning for a number of years.

The twelve Apostles themselves did not come to the full realization of who Jesus was until after the Resurrection and after the Holy Spirit had been poured out upon them on Pentecost Sunday. Once their minds had been enlightened by the Holy Spirit they were able to see implications in things that Jesus had said that were not clear to them at the time he said them. Their recollections of what Jesus had done and said were used in their preaching of the Good News. Eventually that preaching crystallized into definite patterns and form. When the early Christians saw that the Apostles were dying off, they pleaded with them to commit their recollections to writing so that they would be preserved for Christians of future generations. Because of that request we now have the Gospels.

What do the synoptic Gospels tell us about Jesus? They tell us of a man who was aware of his superiority over all creatures, men and angels. He was greater than the prophet Jonah and King Solomon (Matt. 12:41–42), greater than King David who regards him as his Lord (Matt. 22:43ff.). Angels are his servants, for they appear and minister to him (Matt. 4:11), and they will accompany him at his Second Coming (Mark 8:38).

In several New Testament passages Jesus makes himself equal to the Lord God of the Old Testament because he asserts of himself what the Old Testament says about the Lord. Thus, Jesus claims to be superior to the Old Testament Law given through Moses; in his own name he completes and changes certain precepts of the Old Testament Law (Matt. 5: 21ff.). The Jews believed that Yahweh had established the Sabbath worship and rest;

Jesus says that he is Lord of the Sabbath (Luke 6:5) – that is equivalent to claiming to be God.

Aware of his divinity, Jesus imposes obligations on his disciples that only God can require. Thus, he establishes himself as the content and object of faith: "If anyone is ashamed of me and of my words, of him the Son of Man will be ashamed when he comes in his own glory and in the glory of the Father and the holy angels" (Luke 9:20). Moreover, Jesus demands of his followers a love for himself which surpasses all earthly love – something that only God can require: "Anyone who prefers father or mother to me is not worthy of me" (Matt. 10:37).

Jesus is not like other men. Because of his divinity and the infinite depth of his interior life, his disciples do not really understand him. He is fully conscious of his divine power. Who else but God could truly say, "All authority in heaven and on earth has been given to me . . . and lo, I am with you always, to the close of the age" (Matt. 28:18–20). During his public ministry Jesus used his divine power to work many miracles, to raise the dead and to drive out devils. He also communicated that same power to his disciples (Matt. 10:1). Jesus claimed to have the power to forgive sins, which belongs to God alone (Mark 2:5), and proved by his miracles that he really did possess that power (Matt. 9:6).

We all know the beautiful and most perfect prayer, "Our Father." Jesus clearly distinguishes his divine sonship from the adoptive sonship of his disciples. Thus, when he speaks of his relation to his heavenly Father he says, "My Father." When he speaks of the disciples' relation to the Father, he says, "Your Father."

The first revelation of Jesus' unique consciousness of being the Son of God was on the occasion of the Finding in the Temple when he was only twelve years old. He said to his sorrowing parents, "How is it that you sought me? Did you not know that I must be in my Father's house?" (Luke 2:49). Thus, he refers to the Temple in Jerusalem, the most sacred place in Israel, as the "house" of his Father. At the age of twelve there is no doubt that Jesus knows who he is.

In a remarkable passage, Matthew 11:27, Jesus says that "no one knows the Son except the Father, and no one know the Father except the Son." In this statement Jesus made his knowledge equal to the divine knowledge. Jesus also claimed to be the Messiah and the Son of God before the Sanhedrin, as assembly of leading Jewish officials. To the question put to him by the high priest Caiaphas, "I adjure you by the living God, tell us if you are the Christ, the Son of God" (Matt. 26:63), Jesus replied clearly, "You have said so" (26:64). St. Mark records an even more direct answer, "I am he" (Mark 14:62).

There is much evidence in the synoptic Gospels, therefore, that Jesus is and claimed to be true God and the true Son of God.

The divinity of Jesus in St. John's Gospel

The stupendous truth that Jesus of Nazareth is God Almighty in the flesh – the belief of which has changed millions of lives and continues to inspire hundreds of millions of people – is affirmed in the New Testament, in the constant teaching of the Catholic Church throughout the world, and in the sacred liturgy which is celebrated each day by hundreds of thousands of priests.

In the New Testament one of the witnesses who constantly emphasizes the divinity of Jesus is St. John in the Gospel that carries his name. From the Prologue ("In the beginning was the word . . .") in the first chapter to the end of the book the author affirms over and over again that Jesus of Nazareth is the only-begotten Son of God and therefore equal to the Father.

The Gospel of St. John was written about the year 90 A.D. to prove that Jesus is the promised Messiah and the natural Son of God: "These are written that you may believe that Jesus is the Christ, the Son of God, and that believing you may have life in his name" (John 20:31). By the phrase here "Son of God" John means that he is consubstantial with the Father, as we say in the Creed. In order to see this one need only read carefully the first eighteen verses of St. John's first chapter – commonly called the Prologue.

The Prologue begins with a description of the Word who exists from all eternity, who is a distinct Person side by side with God the Father, who is himself God, through whom all finite things were created, who is the source of eternal life (1:1-5). John goes on to say that the Word (Jesus) is "the only Son of the Father" (1:14) and that he entered into the world by becoming flesh. The word "flesh" here is a Semitic way of saying "man" or "human being." The Word made flesh, therefore, is identical with the historical Jesus of Nazareth (1:17–18).

An important part of the proof of Jesus' divinity is what is known in theology as his "pre-existence." By this is meant a number of affirmations, not only in St. John's Gospel but also in the other Gospels and in other books of the New Testament, to the effect that the Second Person of the Blessed Trinity, who became Jesus by uniting to himself a human nature, always existed with the Father *before* he was conceived by the power of the Holy Spirit in the womb of the Virgin Mary. Thus, Jesus says that he was sent into the world by the Father (5:23), that he came "down from heaven" (3:13), that he came from the Father (16:27ff.). In these and in many other statements Jesus asserts his pre-existence with the Father before he became man, not in the sense of a created angel but in the sense of his sonship to God the Father. This makes him equal to the Father and, therefore, asserts his pre-existence from all eternity.

From the New Testament, the Creed, the liturgy, and the teaching of the Church we know and believe that there are three Persons in one God. To say, therefore, that the Son and the Holy Spirit are identical with God or that they are "consubstantial with the Father" is to assert their full divinity. This article of the Creed is based, in part, on a number of affirmations in the Gospel of St. John in which Jesus claims identity with the Father.

There is no doubt that Jesus claimed identity with the Father. Consider, for example, the following two texts: "'My Father is working still, and I am working.' This is why the Jews sought all the more to kill him, because he not only broke the Sabbath but also called God his Father, making himself equal with God" (John 5:17–18). The Pharisees saw clearly that Jesus claimed identity with God; for that reason they wanted to put him to death, since, in their view, he was a blasphemer. Likewise, on another occasion, Jesus said to his enemies, "I and the Father are one" (John 10:30). Here Jesus is speaking about substantial or essential unity with the Father. The Pharisees understood him in that sense, since they accused him of blasphemy and again tried to kill him:

"We stone you for no good work but for blasphemy; because you, being a man, make yourself God" (10:33).

We should also note that Jesus claimed divine qualities for himself. Thus, he said clearly that he is eternal: "Truly, truly I say to you, before Abraham was I am" (8:58). He alone has full knowledge of the Father (7:29), equal power with the Father (5:17ff.) and the power to forgive sins (8:11). Moreover, he calls himself "the light of the world" (8:12) and "the way, the truth, and the life" (14:6). Only God himself can truthfully make such claims.

That Jesus is God is also evident from the fact that he makes divine demands on us by requiring faith in his Person: "You believe in God, believe also in me" (14:1). The reward of faith in Jesus is to be loved by the Father and by Jesus; they will also come to dwell in the hearts of the faithful: "If a man loves me, he will keep my word, and my Father will love him, and we will come to him and make our home with him" (14:23). Only God can do that.

St. John also records the solemn profession of faith in Jesus' divinity by the Apostle Thomas. For when Thomas sees Jesus for the first time after the Resurrection, he exclaims, "My Lord and my God" (20:28). Jesus accepts that as the type of faith that his followers should have in him. In fact, the whole Gospel of St. John was written "that you may believe that Jesus is the Christ, the Son of God, and that believing you may have life in his name" (20:31).

The divinity of Jesus in St. Paul's Letters

Like the synoptic Gospels and St. John, St. Paul, the Apostle to the gentiles, in his letters affirms the divinity of Jesus of Nazareth. For those who have eyes to see and a mind to understand, the letters of St. Paul are shot through with his passionate belief that "Jesus is Lord." I will make reference to some of these passages with the hope that you will take out your New Testament and carefully read some of them for your own spiritual profit. Some of the deepest insights in the Bible regarding who Jesus is are found in the letters of St. Paul. Jesus Christ is the heart and center of the faith and preaching of Paul of Tarsus because he personally experienced the love, beauty, and divine power of Jesus. His whole life was dedicated to persuading others to accept Jesus Christ as their Lord and Master because he knew from divine revelation and therefore was totally convinced that Jesus Christ is the only Savior of all mankind.

One of the clearest expressions of Paul's belief in the divinity of Jesus is contained in Philippians 2:5-11. In the first two verses we read: " Though he was in the form of God, he did not count equality with God a thing to be grasped, but emptied himself, taking the form of a servant." Here the Apostle distinguishes three different levels of Jesus' existence. First, "he was in the form of God," that is, he possessed "equality with God"; then, he took "the form of a servant"; finally, "God has highly exalted him and bestowed on him the name which is above every name" (2:9).

In the New Testament the Greek word for God (*ho theos*) is usually applied only to God the Father, but on a few occasions Paul also says that Jesus is *God*. Thus, while speaking of the many gifts conferred on the Israelites, Paul says: "To them belong the patriarchs, and of their race, according to the flesh, is the Christ, who is God over all, blessed forever" (Rom. 9:5). In writing to

Titus, Paul says that we must "live sober, upright, and godly lives in this world, awaiting our blessed hope, the appearing of the glory of our great *God* and Savior Jesus Christ" (2:13). In Colossians 2:9 Paul says the same thing in a different way: "For in him the whole fullness of deity dwells bodily."

Of the many titles given to Jesus in the New Testament the most important is that of "Lord," the English translation of the Greek "Kyrios." Most Catholics are familiar with this Greek word from the *Kyrie Eleison* of the Latin Mass. Paul constantly refers to Jesus as "the Lord." Thus, he frequently uses such expressions as "the Lord Jesus" or "the Lord Jesus Christ" or simply "the Lord."

Among the Greek-speaking Jews at the time of Jesus, Kyrios was a substitution for the Hebrew God-names Adonai and Yahweh and, as such, was applied to the one true God. According to the witness of St. Paul and the Acts of the Apostles the early Christian communities applied this title to the glorified Jesus after his Resurrection.

In the usage of St. Paul the title "Lord" is equivalent to a confession of the divinity of Jesus Christ. Consider, for example, the following: "At the name of Jesus every knee should bow, in heaven and on earth and under the earth, and every tongue confess that Jesus Christ is Lord, to the glory of God the Father" (Phil. 2:10–11).

One way to prove the divinity of Jesus is to show that the Bible ascribes to him certain qualities or attributes that properly belong to God alone. St. Paul does exactly that. Thus, he attributes divine omnipotence to Jesus: "In him all things were created . . . and in him all things hold together" (Col. 1:15–17). He also ascribes to Jesus omniscience and eternity, qualities, as we have seen, that

20

belong only to God: "In him are hid all the treasures of wisdom and knowledge" (Col. 2:3). According to the First Commandment, worship or adoration is due to God alone, but Paul says that Jesus should be adored: "At the name of Jesus every knee should bow" (Phil . 2:10), and "Let all God's angels worship him" (Heb. 1:6).

So from the titles of "God" and "Lord" that St. Paul attributes to Jesus, and from the divine qualities that he ascribes to him, we can rightly conclude that Paul believed in and proclaimed the divinity of Jesus Christ. That belief alone explains the incredible life of suffering, travel, preaching, and death of the Apostle of the Gentiles.

When we consider the biblical data on the divinity of Father, Son, and Holy Spirit, we should not forget that the New Testament authors did not have all the concepts to work with that we have as the result of two thousand years of reflection and meditation on the life, deeds, and words of Jesus of Nazareth. If all three are God, how are they related to each other? That was a difficult question. Paul defines the relationship of Jesus Christ to God as one of sonship. This sonship, however, is not adoptive, as ours is; it is a true and consubstantial sonship of God, as we profess in the Creed. Thus, Paul says, "God sent his own Son" (Rom. 8:3); God "did not spare his own Son" (Rom. 8:32); and, "He has . . . transferred us to the kingdom of his beloved Son" (Col. 1:13).

These few quotes are just a sample from the letters of St. Paul and offer ample evidence for the assertion that he believed in the full divinity of Jesus Christ the Lord, making him equal to the Father.

In the first centuries of the Christian era there were some thinkers who were so convinced of the divinity of

Jesus that they denied his full humanity, so in the next chapter we will consider the evidence that proves that Jesus is a truly human with a body, soul, and emotions just like all human beings.

Chapter 2
Jesus of Nazareth Is True Man

Having considered Jesus' true divinity, we now move on to a reflection on his true humanity. It may seem strange to some readers that it is necessary to stress the real humanity of Jesus Christ. Most Catholics just assume that Jesus of Nazareth, born in a stable in Bethlehem of the Virgin Mary on Christmas day, is a man just like other men, sin only excepted.

In the course of Church history, however, there have been a number of theological errors, or heresies, that directly concerned the full humanity of Jesus. In the first and second centuries there were heretics called "Gnostics" or "Docetists" who taught that Jesus Christ, the divine Son of God, was only *apparently* a man. They said that he *appeared* to be a man to his disciples and to the crowds as he taught them, but that he did not have a real body such as we have. The reason for this strange view was their belief that matter and the material world are basically evil. They said that the Lord God of the Bible did not create matter; according to them, matter was created by an evil principle or demi-god.

Since, in their view, Jesus is truly God, and since God cannot be touched by evil, and matter is evil, they concluded that God could not become a true man composed of a material body and a soul. Thus, in their view, God revealed himself to us through what appeared to be a man, namely Jesus of Nazareth, but actually he was something like a ghost.

Needless to say, the Church reacted very strongly against this serious error. The Fathers of the Church were tireless in pointing out the many errors that this "Docetism" leads to. "Docetism" is a Greek word which means "appearance." They argued that, if Jesus was not truly a man, then he was not born, he did not suffer, he did not die on the Cross on Calvary. He only *appeared* to do these things. Such a view of Christ destroys all Christian striving for virtue and attempts to follow in the footsteps of Jesus as the way to the Father because it makes him not imitable, not one of us. It undermines all credibility in the historicity of the Bible, since the Gospels recount many concrete details about the life and death of Jesus. Another consequence of Docetism is that it wipes out the validity of the Seven Sacraments, since they use material things such as water, wine, bread, oil; it nullifies the Holy Sacrifice of the Mass and the Real Presence of Jesus in the Eucharist. In effect, it destroys the whole Christian faith and way of life.

For these and many other reasons the Catholic Church has always firmly condemned theories that lead to the denial of the true humanity of Jesus Christ.

The constant faith of the Church is that Jesus, the Second Person of the Trinity and the Word of God, assumed a real human body, not just an apparent body. This is testified to by the most important facts of the earthly life of Jesus, that is, his miraculous conception in the womb of the Virgin Mary, his birth in Bethlehem, his public life, suffering, death, and resurrection.

By reflecting for a moment you will recall that we acknowledge these facts each time we pray the Creed. In the Apostles' Creed we say: "I believe in . . . Jesus Christ, his only Son our Lord, who was *conceived* by the Holy Spirit, *born* of the Virgin Mary, *suffered, died* and was *buried*; he *descended* into hell; the third day he *rose* again from the dead." These statements are all based on the experiences that the Apostles and early disciples had of Jesus during his earthly life; later they were written down and were treasured by succeeding generations of Christians. That is how they came to be part of the Bible as the Gospel according to Matthew, Mark, Luke and John.

Jesus did not merely appear to be a man; by his incarnation the Second Person of the Trinity became one of us. As St. John says in 1:14, "And the Word became flesh and dwelt among us." St. Paul says that he was "born of woman" (Gal. 4:4) and experienced the weaknesses and frailties of human flesh.

Jesus did not just appear to be an infant and a child. Such a thing would be a form of deception and a lie; that is something contrary to the very nature of God who is infinite truth. He grew up into manhood and maturity just as we do: "And Jesus increased in wisdom and in stature, and in favor with God and man" (Luke 2:52).

The Gospels are full of references to the true humanity of Jesus. He was tired and sat down at Jacob's well in Samaria. He slept on the boat on the Sea of Galilee. He wept at the grave of Lazarus. On the way to Calvary, he carried his own cross and was thirsty in his agony. When he died, blood and water flowed from his opened side. After the Resurrection, Jesus assures his doubting disciples of the reality of his human body with the words, "Handle me and see; for a spirit has not flesh and bones as you see that I have" (Luke 24:39).

As you can well imagine, the denial of Jesus' true humanity under the pretense of some "higher spirituality" is a dagger in the heart of the Christian faith. What it really means is that there is no Incarnation, no Redemption and no salvation for mankind. It implies the rejection of the Church, the Sacraments, the Mass and the Real Presence of Jesus in the Blessed Sacrament. It is a heretical attempt on the part of some intellectuals to remove Jesus Christ from the realm of historical reality and transfer him into the area of philosophical speculation. We may rightly apply to them the words of Mary Magdalene at the empty tomb on Easter Morning: "They have taken away my Lord, and I do not know where they have laid him" (John 20:13).

Jesus of Nazareth, the Perfect Man

In order to understand who and what Jesus Christ is according to Catholic faith, it is not sufficient to say that he had a truly human body just like ours. We must also affirm that he had a fully human *soul* just like ours. For if Jesus had only a human body but not a human soul, then he would not really be like us and he would not be our brother. To say that Jesus had a human soul means that he had a human, finite intellect and will like ours. In other words, he possessed the fullness of humanity.

The reason for stressing this point arises because certain heretics, both ancient and modern, have claimed that Jesus did not have a human soul. The famous and influential Arians of the fourth century said that Jesus did not have a human soul and that the Logos or the Word of God took the place of the soul in Jesus. If that were true,

26

it would mean that Jesus was not truly a man like us. The great St. Athanasius spent most of his life fighting the heresy of Arianism, which was condemned in the very first ecumenical Council of Nicaea in 325 A.D.

A variation of Arianism was proposed by Bishop Apollinaris of Laodicea (about 390) which was a city in present day Turkey. Influenced by Platonic philosophy, he taught that the divine Logos had assumed a human body and an animal soul, but that the Logos himself had taken the place of the rational soul in Jesus. He erroneously believed that only in this way could the unity of Person and the sinlessness of Christ be preserved. This theological theory was condemned at a particular or local synod in Alexandria and was rejected as heretical at the First Council of Constantinople in 381.[1]

The great Council of Chalcedon also condemned the view of Apollinaris in 451: "We declare that He [Jesus Christ] is perfect both in his divinity and in his humanity, truly God and truly man composed of body and rational soul; that He is . . . consubstantial with us in his humanity, like us in every respect except for sin" (see Heb. 4:15).[2] That is an infallible statement of the Magisterium of the Church. It is, therefore, an article of Catholic faith that Christ assumed not only a body but also a rational soul endowed with human, finite intellect and will.

There are many indications of this truth in the New Testament. In fact, Jesus speaks of his human soul. Consider, for example, the following: "My soul is very sorrowful, even to death" (Matt. 26:38); "Father, into thy

1   DS 150–151; TCF 12–13.
2   DS 301; TCF 614.

27

hands I commit my spirit!" (Luke 23:46). And all four evangelists report that at his death on the cross Jesus "yielded up his spirit" (Matt. 27:50; Mark 15:37; Luke 23:46; John 19:30).

The human quality of Jesus' soul is manifested in his many prayers of petition and thanksgiving to his heavenly Father; it is shown very clearly in the subordination of his human will to the divine will: "Not my will but thine be done" (Luke 22:42) and "My food is to do the will of him who sent me" (John 4:34).

The Fathers and orthodox theologians of the 4th and 5th centuries argued for the assumption of a rational soul by Christ on the basis of two axioms: "That which has not been assumed has not been saved," and "The Word assumed the flesh through the medium of the soul." The first axiom refers to the redemptive purpose of the Incarnation of the Word; the second refers to the philosophical idea that the soul is the form of the body and that the human body must be informed by a human or rational soul. The problem of how Jesus Christ can be both human and divine is explained by showing that the unity in Christ takes place in the Person of the Word, that is, the Person of the Word exists in two natures, the divine nature and the human nature. Chalcedon defined that there is no mixture or confusion of the two natures in the one Person. This is called the Hypostatic Union.

Another proof for the reality of Jesus' human nature is the fact that he was truly generated and born of a human mother. Through his descent from Mary, a daughter of Adam, he became a son of Adam according to his human nature. Thus, Jesus Christ is truly one of us – he is our brother.

In her various Creeds and other professions of faith the Church teaches that Jesus was generated and born of the Virgin Mary. For example, we pray in the Apostles' Creed that he was "born of the Virgin Mary." The 5tth-century Athanasian Creed puts it this way: "We believe and profess that our Lord Jesus Christ . . . as man was born in time of the substance of His Mother. He is perfect God; and He is perfect man, with a rational soul and human flesh."[3]

The New Testament explicitly stresses the true motherhood of Mary of whom "was born Jesus who is called Christ" (Matt. 1:16). The angel Gabriel said to Mary, "Behold, you will conceive in your womb and bear a son" (Luke 1:31). St. Paul says that when the appointed time came "God sent his Son, *born of woman*" (Gal. 4:4). What is born of a woman is a human child composed of body and soul. Since Jesus was born of a woman, he is fully human with a body and a soul.

It is essential for the very survival of the Church and the Catholic faith that the integral humanity of Jesus Christ be defended and preserved. For, he died for us on the Cross as our brother and Savior. He is also a model for all Christian virtue and living. We follow and imitate the man Jesus Christ on our pilgrimage to the Father.

3   DS 76; TCF 17.

Chapter 3
Jesus Is a Divine Person, Not a Human Person

Having shown that Jesus is both God and man and there-fore has a divine nature and a human nature, the next step is to explain the Church's teaching on how the two natures are joined together in the Person of the Word. When we consider this great mystery we are coming very near to the core or heart of the Christian religion. The Catholic Church, the seven sacraments and the moral life of Christians are based on the amazing reality that Jesus Christ is both God and man – the infinite God in the vis-ibility of human flesh who walked on this earth in Palestine about 2,000 years ago.

The clarity and profundity of the Church's teaching about the unity of the human and divine natures in Christ was occasioned by the false teaching of Nestorius, Patriarch of Constantinople (about 451). Nestorius said that Mary was not the mother of God; according to him she was only the mother of Christ. There are in Christ, he said, two natures and two persons, one divine and one human. According to him, the two persons are connected with each other in moral unity, that is, they agree with each other as any two persons might agree on some proj-ect. According to this theory, the man Jesus is not God, but a very holy man who is the *bearer of God*. The

Incarnation, therefore, does not mean that God the Son became man really, but only that the Divine Logos dwelt in Jesus in the same way that God dwells in the souls of the just by his grace.

According to the Nestorians, the human activities of Jesus (birth, suffering, death) may be asserted of the man Jesus only; the divine activities (creation, omnipotence, omniscience, eternity) may be asserted of the God-Logos only. What this really means is that Mary gave birth to the man Jesus and later the divine Logos came to dwell in him in a special way. That is why the Nestorians said that Mary is the mother of Christ, but not the mother of God.

Under the leadership of St. Cyril of Alexandria (444) the Church reacted strongly against this new teaching. In the General Councils of Ephesus (431) and Chalcedon (451) the Church taught officially and infallibly that the divine and human natures in Jesus Christ are united in one Person – and that Person is the Logos or the Second Person of the Blessed Trinity. Thus, the Church professes that in Jesus there is one Person but two natures – a human nature taken from Mary and the divine nature which is common to Father, Son, and Holy Spirit. Since a mother gives birth not just to a human nature but to a person, it can be said with full truth that Mary is the Mother of God. For the child Mary Gave birth to in Bethlehem is not a human person; he is a divine Person, the Word of God, who has taken to himself a human nature in the womb of the Virgin Mary.

As we have seen, the New Testament offers many proofs that Jesus Christ is both God and man. It attributes to him both divine and human qualities or characteristics (creation, omnipotence, omniscience; birth, suffering, death). Since all of these attributes are affirmed of the one Person, Jesus Christ, it follows that the two natures must belong to the one and the same subject or person.

That Jesus Christ is only one person is especially clear in those texts where the human qualities are predicated of his Person under the title of God, and the divine qualities of his Person are referred to according to his human nature. Thus, we read in John 8:58, "Truly, truly, I say to you, before Abraham was, I am." St. Luke reports that Peter said in Acts 3:15, ". . . you killed the Author of life." St. Paul says in Galatians 4:4, "But when the time had fully come, God sent forth his Son, born of a woman, born under the law."

In this regard it helps to reflect on how Jesus himself uses the first personal pronoun, "I." On one occasion he would say, "I and the Father are one," or "I am the way and the truth and the life," or "I am the bread of life"; on another occasion he would say, "I am thirsty." Both human and divine predicates are affirmed of the same personal subject in Jesus. Thus, the New Testament witnesses to the fact that in Jesus there is only one Person, not two persons.

In her doctrinal teaching the Church has explained this mystery with the phrase "Hypostatic Union." The word "hypostatic" comes from a Greek word which means the same thing as "personal." So what the Church says is that the two natures in Christ, divine and human, are joined together or united in the one Person of the Divine Logos. Jesus therefore is both God and man because he has both a divine nature and a human nature.

The Church affirms the Hypostatic Union as a fact, but she does not explain *how* it is possible for the divine and human natures to be united in the Person of the

Logos or Word of God. That is the mystery of the Incarnation of God; we celebrate that mystery on the feasts of the Annunciation and Christmas. The acceptance and affirmation of this great mystery require an act of faith, not philosophical or theological insight.

The more one reflects on this stupendous mystery, the more one comes to the realization of how much God loves us. He loves us so much that he became one of us in order to save us from sin and death. With the coming of God in Jesus Christ there is no reason for a Christian to be depressed and sad; he should be full of hope and joy because of the presence of Christ in his Church and in the world. For, by becoming man God has made us partakers of the divine nature (2 Pet. 1:4) and destined us for eternal life and eternal happiness if we do his will and remain faithful to him.

Jesus is both God and man

In the 5th century there were some Christians who reacted so strongly against the Nestorian heresy of two persons in Christ that they fell into another error. Under the leadership of a monk in Constantinople by the name of Eutyches (378–454), a group began to stress the oneness or unity of Jesus. They said not only that Jesus is one Person, but they also said that his two natures (divine and human) were fused together by some kind of mixture or composition in order to form one nature. In Greek one is *mono* and nature is *physis*. Thus, in theology these early thinkers are called "Monophysites" and their heresy is called "Monophysitism."

Once again, under the inspiration of the Holy Spirit

and the leadership of the Pope in Rome, the Church reacted strongly and moved to reject this error. For the witness of Scripture and the faith of the Fathers of the Church testified to a different understanding of who and what Jesus is. According to the traditional faith, as we have seen, Jesus Christ is both God and man. He is one divine Person in two natures – the divine nature, and the human nature taken from his mother Mary. The understanding of the Church is that in the Hypostatic Union each of the two natures of Christ continues unimpaired, untransformed, and unmixed with the other. Both natures remain fully intact and come together or are united in the one Person of the Word of God. It is for that reason that we can truthfully say that this man Jesus is God. We can also say with full truth that Mary is the Mother of God because she gave birth to the Second Person of the Blessed Trinity, not of course in his divine nature, but in his created human nature.

In philosophical terms "nature" means the principle of operation of any being; so the powers to act are rooted in the nature. Thus it follows that, if Jesus exists in two natures (divine and human), he must have two kinds of activities. And so it is. By the infinite power of his divine nature he creates, performs miracles, raises Lazarus from the dead, and calms the storm on the Sea of Galilee. By the power of his human nature he walks, talks, eats, sleeps, suffers, and dies. The same Person operates on two levels, but there is perfect unity of the one Person. This is the mystery of the Hypostatic Union and the Incarnation that we profess in faith each Sunday when we pray the ancient Creed of the Church.

It is very important to note that the two natures of Christ are not mixed or confused or divided. Clarity on this matter was established for all time and all generations by the great Council of Chalcedon in 451. I would ask you to read carefully and prayerfully the following infallible pronouncement of that Council:

Following the Holy Father, we all with one accord teach the profession of faith of the one identical Son, our Lord Jesus Christ. We declare that he is perfect both in his divinity and in his humanity, truly God and truly man composed of body and rational soul; that he is consubstantial with the Father in his divinity, consubstantial with us in his humanity, like us in every respect except for sin (Heb. 4:15). We declare that in his divinity he was begotten of the Father before time, and in his humanity he was begotten in this last age of Mary the Virgin, the Mother of God, for us and for our salvation. We declare that the one selfsame Christ, the only-begotten Son and Lord, must be acknowledged *in two natures without any commingling or change or division or separation*; that the distinction between the natures is in no way removed by their union but rather that the specific character of each nature is preserved and they are united in one person and in one hypostasis. We declare that he is not split or divided into two persons, but that there is one selfsame only begotten Son, God the Word, the Lord Jesus Christ. This the prophets have taught about him from the beginning; this Jesus Christ himself taught us; this the creed of the Fathers has handed down to us.[1]

1   DS 301–302; TCF 614–615.

The above doctrine of Chalcedon contains the Church's classic expression of her faith in who Jesus Christ really is. Many important truths of the Catholic faith are contained in the doctrine: for example, that Jesus assumed a real and not just an apparent body; that he had a rational soul with intellect and will like ours; that the two natures in Christ are united in the Person to form one individual; that in Jesus each of the two natures remains unchanged and not mixed or composed with the other; that Jesus is both true God and true man; that Mary is the Mother of God.

It has often been pointed out that the Monophysite doctrine of the unification and fusion of the two natures contradicts the absolute immutability of God. In fact, it also means the denial of the true humanity of Jesus, since if the two natures in him were joined together he would not be human as we are. And we have already seen that such a denial logically leads to a denial of the Church, the sacraments, and our redemption from sin.

The two wills in Christ

There are many important and truly mysterious conse-quences of the Hypostatic Union of two natures in one divine Person. One of them has to do with the number of intellects and wills in Christ. In our experience each per-son has only one intellect and one will. When we look at the beautiful figure of Jesus in the Gospels we see fully a integrated personality. Suppose I put the question to you right now: How many wills are there in Christ? What would your answer be?

When I was teaching a college course on Christ I

36

always asked the students how many wills there are in Christ. In a class of thirty students it was rare to find even one who would answer: "There are two wills in Christ, a divine will and a human will." The usual answer was: "There is one will in Christ because he is one Person." Then I proceeded to point out that they were in serious error with regard to the essential constitution of Jesus Christ our Savior who is both God and man.

A moment's reflection on the great truth of the Hypostatic Union will reveal that there must be two wills in Christ – one divine and one human. Christ is both God and man. That means that he has a divine nature and a human nature. But what is a "nature"? A nature is understood by philosophers and theologians to be a principle of operation. A nature then is active through its powers – it causes things to happen in the real world.

Accordingly, since Jesus possesses two natures, it follows that he must exercise both divine and human activities. What are the activities that are proper to divinity and humanity? They are precisely *thinking* and *willing* which proceed from the spiritual faculties of intellect and will.

No one doubts that Jesus, as a divine Person, possesses divine intellect and will. But he assumed a human nature when he was conceived in the womb of the Blessed Virgin Mary. The theological question here is whether or not he also assumed a human intellect and a human will. Some Christian thinkers of the past have thought that he did not, that the divine intellect and will took the place of the human intellect and will. But that is basically the error of the Monophysites which, as we have seen, was condemned by the Council of Chalcedon in 451. If that position were true, it would follow that Jesus was not truly a human being like us in all things, sin alone excepted.

The infallible teaching of the Church in this matter is that each of the two natures in Christ possesses its own natural will and its own natural mode of operation. Thus there are in Christ two wills and two intellects, a human will and intellect in the human nature and a divine will and intellect in the divine nature. This teaching was sanctioned for all time by the Third Council of Constantinople (680–681): "We promulgate, according to the teaching of the Holy Fathers, that in him are also two natural wills and two natural modes of working, unseparated, untransformed, undivided, unmixed."[2]

According to the New Testament Jesus explicitly distinguishes his human will from his divine will, which he possesses in common with the Father. At the same time, however, Jesus stresses the complete subordination of his human will to his divine will. Thus he prays in Luke 22:42, "Father, if thou art willing, remove this cup from me; nevertheless not my will, but thine, be done."

In a similar vein, Jesus says in John 6:38, "I have come down from heaven, not to do my own will, but the will of him who sent me." Also, Jesus' relation of obedience to his heavenly Father, often stressed in the Bible, presupposes a human will (see for example, John 4:34; Phil. 2:8; Rom. 5:19; Heb. 10:9).

Commenting on Matthew 26:39 (parallel to Luke 22:42) St. Athanasius says: "He announces two wills here, the human, which is an affair of the flesh, and the Divine, which is the affair of God. The human will on account of

2   DS 556; TCF 635.

the weakness of the flesh, prays for the aversion of suffering, but the Divine Will welcomes it."

The Fathers of the Church derive the doctrine of the two wills and modes of activity in Christ from the two natures, divine and human. Will and activity depend on the number of natures, not on the Person. Therefore, since Christ possesses two integral natures, he has two different modes of activity. This means that he has two wills and two intellects, both divine and human.

Chapter 4
The Hypostatic Union

The more we reflect on the incomparable mystery of the Incarnation of the Second Person of the Blessed Trinity, the more we become aware of the infinite love and mercy of God. Many, many questions can be asked about this amazing manifestation of God's love for man. In order to get a little better insight into this mystery it might be helpful to consider the following two questions: When did the Hypostatic Union begin, and how long will it last?

With regard to the beginning of the Hypostatic Union (= union of God and man in the one Person of the Logos: Jesus Christ of Nazareth), two false opinions are worthy of notice. In the third century Origen, influenced by Platonism, said that Christ's human soul pre-existed its union with his body, and was, already before the Incarnation in time, united with the Logos or the Second Person of the Trinity. This opinion was rejected in 543 by Pope Vigilius as false.[1]

Another erroneous view in this matter is that of some of the Gnostics who said that the Logos first descended on the man Jesus on the occasion of his baptism in the Jordan River by St. John the Baptist. This error has reappeared recently in the writing of some biblical scholars

1   DS 403; TCF 401/1.

who maintain that Jesus did not know that he was the Son of God until the Holy Spirit descended on him at his baptism.

The two theories just mentioned run counter to traditional Catholic faith as it is expressed in the Creed of the Church. The Creed asserts the conception as man of the Son of God. Mary did not conceive a human person who later became "Son of God." The latter would have to be correct if the Hypostatic Union of the two natures had occurred at a later point in time. Thus, the Apostles' Creed proclaims, "I believe . . . in Jesus Christ, his only Son our Lord, who was conceived by the Holy Spirit, born of the Virgin Mary."

The New Testament bears witness to the fact that the Son of God became man because he was conceived and born of a woman. Thus, St. Paul says, "But when the time had fully come, God sent forth his Son, born of a woman" (Gal. 4:4; see Rom 1:3).

Another truth to consider is that Mary is the Mother of God, not just the mother of a man. If she had not conceived the Logos in his human nature, then she could not truthfully be called the Mother of God; she would be only the mother of a man. But it is the infallible teaching of the Church, confirmed by the early councils, especially the Council of Ephesus in 431, that Mary is truly the Mother of God (in his human nature). This is another proof that the Hypostatic Union of Christ's human nature with the Second Person of the Trinity took place at the moment of his conception.

Catholic thinkers have also asked whether or not the Hypostatic Union ceased for a time, namely, from the time of his death to his glorious Resurrection. The Apostles' Creed says that the Son of God suffered, was crucified, died, was buried (his body) and descended into hell or the underworld (his soul). Death means the separation of the soul from the body. Since Christ truly died, it follows that his soul was separated from his body from the moment of his death until his Resurrection. The question arises whether or not the Logos remained united to the body and the soul during those three days. It is a common teaching of Catholic theologians that the divine Logos remained hypostatically united to both the body and the soul after Jesus' death. This means that Jesus' body in the tomb on Holy Saturday was still united to the Logos and therefore worthy of full adoration.

Some Gnostic heretics have maintained that the Logos abandoned Jesus before his passion. By this they mean that the hypostatic Union ceased before he began to suffer. But the Hypostatic Union did not cease before or after the passion. This is shown by the statement of St. Paul, "If they had known the concealed wisdom of God they would never have crucified the Lord of Glory" (1 Cor. 2:8).

The Gnostics try to prove their point by quoting Matthew 27:46, "My God, my God, why hast thou forsaken me?" There is no doubt that this passage has troubled many devout Christians. St. Thomas Aquinas and other theologians explain it in the sense that the Father withdrew certain aspects of his protection of Jesus, but not that the Logos abandoned Jesus. Here Jesus experiences the depths of human suffering and anguish, but he is and remains the Son of God.

Another questions that suggests itself in this connection is whether or not the divine Logos, after the end of the world and the judgment of the living and the dead, will cast off his human nature and cease to be hypostatically united to flesh and blood. In the past some have also held this opinion, but it was rejected as heretical by the First Council of Constantinople in 381. In order to make sure that this error did not recur the Council ordered the following addition to the Creed that we pray at Mass, "and his Kingdom will have no end." Another indication that the Hypostatic Union will continue for all eternity is contained in the words of the angel Gabriel to Mary: "The Lord will give to him [= Jesus] the throne of his father David, he will reign over the house of Jacob for ever" (Luke 1:32–33).

Understanding the Hypostatic Union

In order to learn more about our Catholic faith, it is most important to understand clearly what the Church means by the expression, *Hypostatic Union*. The correct understanding of the Catholic faith, and indeed of Jesus Christ, depends directly on the meaning of this phrase.

The word "hypostatic" comes from the Greek "hypostasis" and it means "personal." The expression "Hypostatic Union" was developed by the early Fathers of the Church to describe the mystery-laden union of the divine and human natures in the one Person, Jesus Christ.

We all know what it means to be a person because that is what we are. But it is not at all easy to describe it or to explain it. The philosophers say that it is the ultimate subject of predication. Thus, whatever is said about "me" refers to the "I" in me. Each and every human being is also a human person. In our daily experience person and human nature always go together. Animals, plants. and minerals do not qualify as persons because they are lacking in intelligence and free will – the two attributes that are characteristic of persons. Because persons have free will, only they can be held morally responsible for their actions.

From divine revelation we know that angels and devils exist and that they too are personal beings. In the most perfect sense God is personal being. Here again we know, but only from revelation, that what we mean by "person" is found multiplied in God, that is, God is a Trinity – three Persons in one God – Father, Son, and Holy Spirit.

When the Church uses the expression "Hypostatic Union" to describe the great mystery of the Incarnation of God or God becoming man, she is telling us that Jesus' human nature is united with his divine nature in the one Person of the Word or Second Person of the Blessed Trinity. This means that Jesus is not a human person, but a divine Person. This has been mentioned in a previous section, but I wish to emphasize it here.

The consequence of this is that in virtue of the Hypostatic Union Jesus is both God and man at the same time. Here is how the famous Athanasian Creed of the fifth or sixth century puts it:

> As God He was begotten of the substance of the Father before time; as man He was born in time of the substance of His mother. He is perfect God; and He is perfect man, with a rational soul and human flesh. He is equal to the Father in His divinity but He is inferior to His Father in his humanity. Although He is God and man, He is not two but one Christ. And He is one, not because His divinity was changed into flesh, but

because his humanity was assumed to God. He is one, not at all because of a mingling of substances, but because He is one person.[2]

This of course is the central mystery that surrounds the Person of Jesus Christ – how can he be both God and man at the same time. Revelation tells us that the Word of God became man in Jesus Christ (John 1:14), but it does not tell us *how* that was accomplished.

The more we reflect on the Hypostatic Union, the more we realize that the assumption of a created human nature into the unity of a divine person is absolutely supernatural. It is a *grace* in the full sense of that word, that is, an unmerited and unmeritable supernatural gift of God. The scholastic theologians refer to it as "the grace of union."

The Hypostatic Union is an absolute mystery of faith; so also is the Holy Trinity. An absolute mystery is one whose reality could not be known before its divine revelation; even after its revelation one cannot prove the intrinsic possibility of an absolute mystery of faith. Accordingly, it is beyond the power of human reason, but, since it has been revealed by God who is absolute truth, it is not contrary to reason. St. Paul calls the Incarnation "the mystery hidden for ages in God" (Eph. 3:9).

The Incarnation and the Trinity

There is an essential connection between the Incarnation and the Trinity since, according to our faith, Jesus Christ

2   DS 76; TCF 17.

is the Second Person of the Blessed Trinity. Careful readers of the New Testament will have noted that Holy Scripture attributes the Incarnation (or Hypostatic Union) to the Father (Heb. 10:5), to the Son (Phil. 2:7), and to the Holy Spirit (Matt. 1:18, 20; Luke 1:35). A question I would like to treat now is this: Who caused or brought about the Incarnation of the Word of God? The Bible attributes it to each of the three divine persons.

The official teaching of the Church is that the Incarnation or Hypostatic Union was effected by the three divine persons acting in common. An important Creed from the seventh century says on this point: "It should be believed that the whole Trinity effected the Incarnation of this Son of God, because the works of the Trinity cannot be divided."[3] The Fourth Lateran Council in 1215 said the same thing: "The only begotten Son of God, Jesus Christ, was made incarnate by a common action of the Holy Trinity."[4]

The basic reason for this Catholic teaching is that the divine nature, which is common to the three divine persons, is and must be the active principle of all operations, such as creation, which take place outside of the inner Trinitarian life. The Incarnation of the Son of God in space and time is just such an activity. Therefore, it is common to the Father, Son, and Holy Spirit. Accordingly, in different contexts the New Testament attributes the Incarnation to each of the three divine persons.

A little reflection on the Incarnation will reveal that it must be the work of the whole Trinity. For the Trinity of Persons is also a unity of nature; there is only one God in

3   DS 535; TCF 630.
4   DS 801; TCF 20.

three divine persons. But the divine persons do not act as separate individuals; they are not like human persons, each with his or her own nature. Everything they do in the created world is common to all three persons. Thus, St. Augustine says: "Mary's conceiving and bringing forth is the work of the Trinity, through whose creative activity all creation is made."

Another point I would like to make is that only the second divine Person became man; he is also called the Son of God or the Word or the Logos. Stated negatively, this means that the Father and the Holy Spirit were not incarnated.

In this difficult theological matter, one might be tempted to think that the whole Trinity was incarnated in Jesus of Nazareth. Since Father, Son, and Holy Spirit act in common in the created world, it might seem that, if one person becomes man, then all of them become man. Some of the early heretics actually held that erroneous opinion, but they were condemned by various Church councils. For the New Testament refers to the Son of God *only* when it says that he became flesh and dwelt among us (John 1:14). The Creed says clearly that only the Son of God "came down from heaven . . . was born of the Virgin Mary, and became man."

Since the high middle ages there has been considerable speculation among Catholic theologians about whether or not the Father and the Holy Spirit could be incarnated, that is, assume a human nature and so become man. Some theologians have been of the opinion that any divine person could become man.

In recent years, however, this opinion has become less common. Most contemporary dogmatic theologians would hold that only the Second Person of the Blessed

Trinity, the Son of God, could become man. The reason for this opinion is that the incarnate God is the revelation, the visibility of the infinite and invisible God. The Incarnation is a manifestation of God to personal beings endowed with intelligence and free will. In a very true sense the God-man Jesus Christ leads us to the Father; his is the *image* of the Father (see John 14:9). Now we know from Catholic doctrine about the Trinity that the Father generates the Son and that the Son is therefore the image or reflection of the Father. He is the expression of the Father.

The incarnate God-man, therefore, is the external expression of God. Since the Second Person of the Trinity is by nature the *image* of the Father, the *Word* of God, it would seem that only he could become man and thus become the visibility and revelation of God.

Jesus Christ deserves adoration

Since the Person in Jesus Christ is the Second Person of the Blessed Trinity, this means that he is both God and man – he has both a divine nature and a human nature. He is also the visibility of God in the material world. What does this mean for our relationship toward him? Since he is God and we are poor creatures, and since the creature is required by nature to show respect and adoration for its Creator and God, it follows that Jesus Christ has the right to our respect and adoration.

In the history of the Church the question has often been raised about whether or not Jesus should be revered and honored as a holy man, or whether he should be adored as God Almighty, with the same adoration that we offer to God the Father.

Some have held that as God Jesus was the natural Son of God and as man he was the adopted son of God. They said that in the baptism in the Jordan River Jesus was adopted by God through grace. This theory of a double sonship in Jesus Christ implies that there are two persons in him, one divine and one human. This is the error of Nestorianism which has been condemned by the Church many times because it implies a denial of the Incarnation. The Church has defined infallibly that there is only one Person in Jesus and that Person is the Logos or Word of God. This means that not only as God, but also as man, Jesus Christ is the natural Son of God. Therefore we owe him the worship due to God alone because he is God.

"Worship" is a kind of honor or esteem given to a person because of his excellence. In religious matters, worship adds to honor or esteem the sense of one's own inferiority with regard to the person honored. Since God is the supreme being, worship in the highest degree is due to him. The correct name for this type of worship is "adoration." The Latins and Greeks called it *latria*, which meant the service given to the gods. That word makes up the second part of the English word "idolatry."

The teaching of the Catholic Church in this matter is that the God-man Jesus Christ is to be venerated with the one single mode of worship – the absolute worship of adoration, which is due to God alone. Jesus Christ is one divine Person subsisting in a divine nature and a human nature. He is therefore *One*. Adoration of Jesus is adoration of the Second Person of the Blessed Trinity by reason of the Hypostatic Union, which has already been explained. Through the Hypostatic Union Christ's humanity is a part of and belongs to the incarnate Logos and so is adored in and with the Logos. The human nature of Christ is clearly a creature but it is still the object of our adoration, not because it is a creature, but because of its Hypostatic Union with the Logos.

There are several instances related in the Gospels in which individuals worship Jesus by kneeling before him (Matt. 28:9, 17). Jesus also claims for himself the same veneration which is due to the Father: ". . . that all may honor the Son, even as they honor the Father" (John 5:23). St. Paul witnessed to the divine adoration owed to Christ in his humanity: ". . . that at the name of Jesus every knee should bow, in heaven and on earth and under the earth" (Phil. 2:10).

Some early heretics accused the Church of adoring just the flesh of Christ or simply the man Jesus. The Fathers of the Church rejected the charges on the ground that adoration is shown to Christ's humanity, not on its own account and as something separated from the Word, but on account of its Hypostatic Union with the Second Person of the Blessed Trinity.

In the proper sense, veneration is shown to a person only. There is only one divine Person in Christ, so we offer him one adoration only. Since the human nature of Jesus Christ is inseparably united with the divine Person of the Word, adoration directed to that divine Person must include the human nature. St. Thomas Aquinas sums up this matter in the following words: "The honor of adoration belongs in the proper sense to the subsisting person. . . . The adoration of Christ's flesh means nothing else than the adoration of the Word become Flesh."[5]

What this means in the realm of the liturgy is that by adoring Christ we are adoring the incarnate Word.

5 *Summa Theologiae* III, q. 25, art 2.

Christ's human nature is included in our adoration because it is hypostatically and eternally united to the Second Person of the Blessed Trinity. The fundamental reason for our adoration is the infinite perfection, being, and beauty of the divine Person. Thus, when we adore Christ we are adoring God Almighty because Jesus Christ is God.

Adoration of the Heart of Jesus

If adoration is due to the whole Christ, one can raise a question about the individual parts of his body. May we, and should we, adore certain parts of Jesus' sacred humanity? Why raise this question? Well, there is an ancient Catholic tradition of showing special veneration or adoration for individual parts of Jesus' human nature – for the Five Holy Wounds, for the Most Precious Blood, for the Holy Face, for his Most Sacred Heart. The Church has approved of these devotions for centuries. The reason for the special veneration of these parts of Jesus' human nature is found in the fact that in them the redeeming love of Christ is revealed very clearly.

We can say with certainty that, just as adoration is due to the whole human nature of Christ, so also is it due to the individual parts of his nature. For they are all hypostatically united to the Person of the Word. For our present consideration I wish to apply this principle to the Sacred Heart of Jesus. Thus, just as we ought to adore the whole humanity of Christ, so we may and we ought to adore the Heart of Jesus Christ. That Heart is a symbol of the divine and human love that Jesus has for each one of us.

Devotion to the Sacred Heart of Jesus originated with

the German mystics of the Middle Ages. It has its scriptural foundation in John 19:34, "One of the soldiers pierced his side with a spear, and at once there came out blood and water." Pope Pius VI declared in 1794 that the Heart of Jesus is not separated from the Godhead, but rather is adored as "the heart of the Person of the Word, with which it is inseparably united."

When we worship the Heart of Christ, what precisely do we worship? Is our worship directed to the physical Heart of Jesus? Or do we worship the divine love for us and use the Heart of Jesus merely as a symbol for that love? It may surprise some, but the object of the devotion is the corporeal Heart of Jesus, as an essential part of the human nature of Christ which is hypostatically united to the Person of the Word. We worship the Heart of Jesus because it is the Heart of God, the Second Person of the Blessed Trinity.

Jesus' Heart has been singled out for special veneration because the heart is the most perfect symbol of his redeeming love for mankind. Both in the Bible (see Deut. 6:5; Prov. 2:2; Matt. 22:37; John 16:6, 22; Rom. 5:5) and in popular language the heart is the center of our affections, especially the affection of love. Since God's love is the motive of our redemption (see John 3:16), special love and adoration are shown to the physical Heart of Jesus our Redeemer because it is the symbol of his love for us.

The purpose of the devotion to the Sacred Heart of Jesus is that we will be moved to return love for love, to imitate the virtues of the human Heart of the incarnate God, and to promote a desire to atone for the insults offered by men to the Heart of Jesus.

It is regrettable that devotion to the Sacred Heart of Jesus has declined so much among Catholics since

Vatican II. For, this devotion touches the very roots of Christianity. Ultimately, what life and religion are all about is love. Through human love we get a taste of absolute, divine love. In Christ Jesus the love of God for man is fully revealed. There is no better symbol of God's infinite love for sinful mankind than the physical Heart of the God-man Jesus Christ.

"Heart" is a universally understood symbol of love. Thus, when we speak of the Heart of Jesus we are referring to the boundless love of God's only-begotten Son for us. By honoring the Heart of Jesus we are directly honoring the love of the Second Person of the Blessed Trinity for man; we are also, through Jesus, honoring the love of the Father and the Holy Spirit for us.

Prayer and love are major concerns of Catholics today. A rightly understood and practiced devotion to the love of Jesus Christ can satisfy that concern to the highest degree. Devotion to the Sacred Heart of Jesus has been highly recommended by the last fifteen popes. Pius XI called it "the synthesis of all religion, the norm of the more perfect life." Pius XII said that it is "a most perfect way of professing the Christian religion." In a time of growing cynicism, despair, violence, and atheism there is no better way to live the fullness of the Catholic faith, it seems to me, than by consecrating oneself to the Heart of Jesus, which the Litany of the Sacred Heart refers to as "the burning furnace of love."

Talking about Jesus

A further consequence of the Hypostatic Union concerns the way in which we talk about Jesus. Careful analysis of

53

the New Testament reveals that both human and divine attributes or qualities or properties are predicated of him. Since Jesus Christ is both God and man, it follows that we can attribute to him both divine and human qualities. In this we are merely following the example of the Bible.

If you can run over in your mind the first part of the Apostles' Creed you will note that it attributes to the Son of God the human properties of conception and birth, of suffering and crucifixion, of dying and being buried. The Bible and the Church also attribute divine qualities to Jesus Christ, such as divinity, creation, eternity. Some of the ancient heretics, called Nestorians, said there are two persons in Christ – one human and one divine. They said, falsely, that the human qualities belonged to the human person in Jesus and that the divine qualities belonged to the divine Person in Jesus. The Council of Ephesus in 431, however, taught that the biblical statements about Christ may not be divided between two persons, the Word of God and the human Christ, but must be referred to the one Word made flesh.

It must be remembered that Christ's divine Person exists in two natures, one divine and one human, and that it may be referred to either of these two natures. This means, therefore, that human things can be asserted of the Son of God and divine things of the Son of Man.

Perhaps a few examples from the New Testament will help to make this difficult teaching of the Bible and the Church more clear. We read in John 8:58, "Before Abraham was, I am" (the man-Christ). In Acts 3:15 St. Peter says to the people of Jerusalem, "You killed the author of life." In Acts 20:28 St. Paul tells the elders of Ephesus "to care for the church of God which he obtained with the blood of his Son." And Paul writes in 1 Corinthians 2:8, "None of the rulers of this age understood this; for if they had, they would not have crucified the Lord of glory" (i.e., God). In these passages we find both divine and human predicates attributed to Jesus Christ. The reason for this is that whatever is true of either the divine nature or the human nature of Jesus Christ can truthfully be said of him because the subject of the predication is the Person of the Word.

To say that the Lord of Glory has been crucified seems to be a contradiction. For, how can God, the Lord of Glory, possibly undergo crucifixion? The answer is that he cannot in his divine nature, but he can in his passible human nature. Both natures are united in the one Person of the Word. Since the man Jesus is a divine Person, the Fathers of the Church, basing themselves on Holy Scripture, were bold enough to speak of the blood of God, the sufferings of God and the birth of God from Mary.

Qualities pertaining to both the divine and the human nature can be attributed to the Person of Christ, but it is to be noted that qualities belonging specifically to one nature cannot be said of the other nature. Thus, it is true to say that the Son of Man died on the Cross and that Jesus created the world. In both cases the activity is referred to the one Person of Christ. But it would be false to say, "Christ suffered as God." For Christ suffered in his human nature, not in his divine nature, which is not capable of suffering. Likewise, it would be false to say, "Christ as man created the world." He did create the world, but not "as man": he created it as God.

For the same reasons it would be false to say, "Christ's soul is omniscient," or "Christ's body is everywhere."

We must beware of negative statements about Jesus

since nothing may be denied to Jesus Christ which belongs to him according to either nature. Thus, it is false to say, "The Son of God has not suffered," or "Jesus is not divine." In order to be perfectly clear it is helpful to add qualifications like "as God" or "as man," depending on which nature is being referred to. Thus, for example, it is correct to say, "Christ, as man, is a creature."

The two natures of Jesus Christ, despite the real distinction between them, do not exist side by side but are in a most close and intimate union. From the mysterious Hypostatic Union there derives a mutual intimate union and penetration of one nature by the other. The power which unites the two natures and holds them together proceeds exclusively from the divine nature. The divinity, which itself is impenetrable, penetrates and inhabits the humanity, which is thereby deified without suffering any change.

In conclusion, I would like to point out that Christianity is the only religion on earth that has a clear idea of a true incarnation of God and which the Catholic Church defines with the expression "Hypostatic Union." This is a truth that surpasses the capability of every created intellect, and its reality was revealed only by the Word made flesh, namely, by Jesus of Nazareth. In one of his articles St. Thomas Aquinas has this to say about the Incarnation: "Indeed, among divine works, this most especially exceeds the reason: for nothing can be thought of which is more marvelous than this divine accomplishment: the true God, the Son of God, should become true man. And because among them all it is the most marvelous, it follows that toward faith in this particular marvel all other miracles are ordered, since 'that which is greatest in any genus seems to be the cause of the others.'"[6] Thus, from this point of view it is clear that Jesus Christ is the heart and center of the whole supernatural order.

In the attempt to understand this marvelous mystery better, saints and theologians have tried to find some analogies to it from the things of nature. St. Thomas said that the union of the soul with the body of the human person has a certain similarity to the Hypostatic Union.[7] This unique union has also been compared to the grafting of a sprig into a mature tree and with the spiritual marriage between the Word and humanity. These are only weak analogies that have some relation to the mystery, but they do not explain it because the Incarnation of God is an absolute mystery that surpasses the mental capability of any and every created intellect, including that of the Blessed Virgin Mary and the angels in heaven.

6   *Summa Contra Gentiles* IV, 27.
7   *Summa Contra Gentiles* IV, 41:9–10.

Chapter 5
The Knowledge of Jesus

The Hypostatic Union had a profound effect on Jesus' human nature. As we have seen, Jesus Christ is a true man, but, because he is also God, he is no ordinary man. He is like us in all things except sin, but he is also unlike us in that his human nature is hypostatically united to the Word of God. It is important to remember that Jesus is not a human person like us; he is a divine Person – the Second Person of the Blessed Trinity. Because of the Hypostatic Union, Jesus' human nature was endowed with an abundance of supernatural gifts; in fact, he has the perfection of all the virtues. This raises questions about his human knowledge, human will, and human power. Here I would like to make a few points about Jesus' human knowledge.

There is an ancient tradition in the Church, going back to the early Fathers, that the human soul of Jesus possessed the immediate or Beatific Vision of God from the first moment of his existence in the womb of his mother, the Virgin Mary. The immediate vision of God is absolutely supernatural; it is granted to the angels in heaven and to the saints in heaven. What the Fathers and theologians have said and say is that Christ's soul possessed the immediate vision of God from the first moment of its union with the divine Person of the Word, that is, from its conception in Mary. This means that Jesus was, at the same time, both a pilgrim on earth like us and a possessor of the immediate vision of God like the blessed in heaven. One of the consequences of his immediate vision of God is that he did not have the theological virtues of faith and hope, since faith and hope cease once there is vision and possession of God.

Over the centuries there have been many theological disputes about the human knowledge of Christ. Thus, in 1918 Pope Benedict XV declared that the following three propositions cannot be taught safely by a Catholic:

1) It is not certain that there was in the soul of Christ, during his life among men, the knowledge possessed by the blessed or those in glory.

2) Equally uncertain is the statement which claims that the soul of Christ was ignorant of nothing, but that from the beginning it knew in the Word all things, past, present, and future; in a word, that it knew all things which God knows by the knowledge of vision.

3) The position of some recent spokesmen about the limited knowledge of the soul of Christ should be no less acceptable to Catholic schools than the statement of the ancients about its universal knowledge.[1]

Please note that the Pope says the above statements cannot be taught safely. That means that the opposite is closer to the truth, namely, that Jesus had the immediate vision of God, that he knows all things – past, present and future, and that his human knowledge is unlimited in some respects.

There are several indications in the New Testament that Jesus has immediate knowledge of the Father. Thus, we read in John 1:17–18, ". . . grace and truth came

1   DS 3645–3647; TCF 651/1–3.

through Jesus Christ. No one has ever seen God; the only Son, who is in the bosom of the Father, he has made him known." Jesus also says in John 8:55, "I know him [the Father]. If I said, I do not know him, I should be a liar like you; but I do know him and I keep his word."

That Jesus had the Beatific Vision from the moment of his conception is a conclusion that the Fathers of the Church and theologians like St. Thomas Aquinas arrived at by examining who and what Jesus is. The Beatific Vision is the consummation of sanctifying grace; also, the attachment of the soul to God through grace and glory is an accidental union or perfection of the created soul. The attachment of Christ's soul to God, however, is a substantial union because it is hypostatically united to the Word of God. Such a substantial union is more intimate than the union of the saints in heaven with God. Thus, if Christ's soul on earth was already more intimately united to God than the blessed are in heaven, it follows that it must have at least the same immediate knowledge of God that the saints and angels have.

St. Thomas also argues that, since Christ by his life and death is the source of salvation and heaven for all mankind, he must have what he gives to others. Since he communicates the Beatific Vision to others, he must have it himself because no one can give what he does not have.

According to Hebrews 12:2, Jesus "leads us in our faith and brings it to perfection." If he leads us and perfects us in faith, then he knows perfectly what he is doing and does not himself walk in the darkness of faith, as I mentioned above. The perfection of the knowledge and self-consciousness of the man Jesus can be explained only by the fact that he possessed immediate knowledge of the divinity with which he was substantially united.

In concrete terms this means that Jesus' soul had the immediate vision of God from the first moment of its existence. He already had in this life what we hope to attain in the next life.

Vision and suffering

In the Beatific Vision Jesus saw everything that pertained to his mission as Redeemer of the world. He saw you and me; he saw all of our deeds and knew all our thoughts. How could this not be, since the Father has established him as our Eternal Judge?

The reality of Jesus' Beatific Vision raises a number of difficult and fascinating questions about his human knowledge and his ability really to suffer, especially in his passion. For the immediate vision of God causes supreme happiness in rational creatures, such as angels and men. If that is so, and if Jesus possessed the Beatific Vision during all his life, how can that be reconciled with his profound sorrow during his agony in the Garden of Gethsemane? And how can it be reconciled with his cry of agony on the cross? Can both beatitude and extreme suffering be present in Jesus at the same time?

These are very difficult questions which touch immediately on the mystery of Christ, the mystery of the Incarnation of God. The classical explanation of the difficultly was given by St. Thomas Aquinas and has been adopted, in one form or another, by most theologians since his time. He made a distinction between the spiritual powers of the soul and the sensitive powers of the soul. By a special divine ordinance, he said, the joy deriving from the Beatific Visions was limited in Christ to his spiritual soul. According to Thomas, the overflow of bliss into the body does not belong to the nature of glory; it is an accidental consequence of it, which was suspended by God in the special case of Jesus Christ during his earthly life. There was a brief exception to this, however, during his Transfiguration on Mount Tabor, when the divine glory shone through his body.

Thus, since by the miraculous intervention of God the bliss proceeding from the immediate vision of God did not overflow from the higher powers of the soul to the lower, nor from the soul to the body, Jesus remained sensitive to sorrow, sadness, and suffering. How this was accomplished remains ultimately mysterious, since we are dealing with the mystery of the Incarnation, but at least it offers some explanation.

In this difficult matter we must hold on to two truths: 1) Jesus had the Beatific Vision during his whole life and passion; 2) Jesus truly suffered both in body and soul. The witness of the four Gospels is clear that Jesus truly suffered not only physically but also mentally. "And he said to them: 'My soul is very sorrowful, even unto death; remain here, and watch'" (Mark 14:34). "And at the ninth hour Jesus cried out with a loud voice, 'Elo-i, Elo-i, lama sabach-thami?' which means, "My God, my God, why hast thou forsaken me?'" (Mark 15:34).

The mystery seems to be that, even though Jesus possessed perfect psychological unity, he could enjoy the Beatific Vision in one part of his soul and suffer intense agony and abandonment by God in another part of his soul.

It has already been pointed out that Jesus Christ is a divine Person, not a human person, with two natures – the divine nature and a human nature. This means in the concrete that Jesus has two intellects (divine and human) and two wills (divine and human). The reason for this is that nature is the principle of operation in any being. This also means that Jesus had a divine consciousness and a human consciousness – both united in the one Person of the Word. It is very difficult, and probably impossible, for us to imagine how two consciousnesses can achieve psychological unity. Nevertheless, our faith does affirm that Jesus possessed that psychological unity.

The Gospels present Jesus as a Person who is fully integrated, wise, self-possessed, with a perfect knowledge of the Father and his relationship to the Father. Since he revealed the Father and the Holy Spirit to us, he had an intimate knowledge of them that comes only from union and vision.

Thus, our Catholic faith urges us to hold fast to these two truths: Jesus enjoyed the immediate vision of God during his earthly life; he also truly suffered for us both in his body and his soul.

Did ignorance or error exist in Christ?

We have been considering some of the effects of the Hypostatic Union in the soul and body of Jesus. One consequence of that mysterious, unique union was that Jesus possessed the Beatific Vision of God from the first moment of his conception. The primary object of that vision of God is the divine essence – that is what Jesus saw with his human intellect. Because of the finiteness of human nature, however, Jesus as man did not have a *comprehensive* knowledge of God. That means that Jesus' human mind did not know everything knowable about

God. For, the finite cannot contain the infinite and the intellect of Jesus Christ is a finite entity. No finite intellect – not the Blessed Virgin Mary nor any of the angels – can comprehend the infinite God. Only God knows himself completely or comprehensively.

The secondary object of the immediate vision of God is found in those things that are external to God and are seen in him as the origin of all things. The extent of this kind of knowledge depends on the perfection with which God is known; that perfection for each saint in heaven depends on the level of grace each one had at the moment of death. For the angels and saints in heaven it includes the knowledge of those things that pertain to them, for example, knowledge of family members and friends.

Because of the Hypostatic Union, Christ's soul is more closely united to God than are the angels and saints. Therefore, he knew everything that pertained to him and to his mission as the Redeemer of the world and as the Teacher of the way to salvation. Thus, during his earthly life Christ's soul knew all extra-divine things in the divine essence, to the extent that such knowledge was necessary for his mission as Redeemer. St. Thomas concluded that, since Christ is the Lord of all creation and the Eternal Judge of all mankind, his soul knew in the divine essence all real things of the past, present and future, including the thoughts of all men of all times.[2]

The limitation on Christ's human knowledge was that he did not know all the possible things that God could do. The way theologians explain it, that kind of knowledge is equivalent to comprehensive knowledge:

2 *Summa Theologiae* III, q. 10, art. 2.

only God knows himself in that way. No created intellect of angel or man can have comprehensive knowledge of God, not even Christ's human soul.

Christ's soul therefore possessed, as St. Thomas says, a relative omniscience, not an absolute one. He knew all real things – past, present, and future. In order to protect this truth, the Holy See in 1918 in the time of Pope Benedict XV rejected the following proposition: "Nor can the opinion be said to be certain which holds that Christ's soul was not ignorant of anything but from the beginning knew in the Word all things past, present, and future, that is, everything that God knows with the knowledge of vision."[3]

It follows then that Christ's human knowledge was free of all ignorance and error. Let us look at the New Testament. Jesus calls himself "the light of the world" (John 8:12), which came into the world to bring true knowledge to mankind (John 12:46). He calls himself "the truth" (John 14:6), and says that he came into the world to give testimony to the truth (John 18:37). In him are hidden "all the treasures of wisdom and knowledge " (Col. 2:3). He knows things that take place far away (John 1:48), and he sees through the heart of man (John 1:47; 2:24ff.; 6:71). The idea that Jesus' knowledge was defective in any way, or that he was in error about some things, cannot be reconciled with these statements of the Bible.

Among the ancient heretics there were some who said that Jesus was ignorant of many things; others said that he was in error on some points, especially about the Parousia and the end of the world. The text that

3   DS 3646; TCF 651/2.

occasioned much dispute on this point is Mark 13:32, which refers to the Second Coming of Christ: "But of that day or that hour no one knows, not even the angels in heaven, nor the Son, but only the Father." The problem arises because Jesus said that "the Son," namely himself, does not know when the Parousia will occur.

The Fathers of the Church attempted a number of different explanations of the text. The explanation of St. Augustine is the one that was generally adopted. He said that Christ, in his human intellect, possessed divine knowledge that was communicable and non-communicable. In other words, what pertained to his mission as Redeemer he could communicate to us; what did not pertain to that mission was non-communicable knowledge. Thus, it was not in accordance with the Father's will that Jesus reveal when the end of the world will take place (see Acts 1:7). St. Augustine says, "It was not part of his teaching duty to make it [the Day of Judgment] known to us."

In all of this it is important to remember that the basic reason for the impossibility of ignorance or error in Christ's human soul is found in the most mysterious Hypostatic Union. For, it is irreconcilable with the dignity of the divine Person to ascribe to him such imperfections.

Jesus' infused and acquired knowledge

For many centuries theologians have been arguing about the nature and extent of Jesus' human knowledge. We have already seen that he possessed the Beatific Vision from the first moment of his conception in the womb of his Virgin Mother. A further question has been raised about whether or not there was also in his intellect infused knowledge. It is an accepted point in Catholic teaching that the angels do not learn from experience as we do; they do not have bodies and sense faculties as we do, so they do not have sense experience. Their knowledge was given to them by God, or infused into them, at the moment of their creation.

We human beings come into this world with certain faculties or powers of learning, but we do not have any actual knowledge. This comes from experience of the world around us. At birth our minds are a blank, a *tabula rasa,* as the saying goes. Must we say then that Christ came into this world lacking all knowledge just like all human beings? Or did he possess certain gifts of knowledge because of the Hypostatic Union and because he was the Redeemer of the world?

It has been the common teaching of most theologians since St. Thomas Aquinas that, from the beginning of his existence, Jesus' soul possessed infused knowledge. By "infused knowledge" is meant spiritual concepts and ideas which are immediately and habitually communicated to the mind by God. Thus, infused knowledge does not depend on sense experience in its acquisition. There seem to be many examples of this kind of knowledge in the lives of prophets like St. John the Baptist and great mystics like St. Teresa of Avila who have been illuminated about divine things directly by God.

It is not possible to offer a strict proof from Scripture for this kind of knowledge in Jesus Christ, but there are some indications of it. Thus, for example, St. Paul says of him that "in him are hid all the treasures of wisdom and knowledge" (Col 2:3). He is also called the Wisdom of God (1 Cor. 1:24) and the Mystery of God (1 Cor. 2:7).

St. Thomas says that the dignity of the human nature assumed by the Word of God requires that it should lack no perfection which human nature is capable of. That would seem to require the perfection of human knowledge. Also, since he is the Head of all creation and the Teacher of mankind about eternal life, it seems appropriate that he should not be lacking in any knowledge. Moreover, as the Revealer of the intimate secrets of God, such as the Trinity and God's plan for mankind, it seems fitting that Jesus Christ should know all things, past, present, and future. This knowledge he received directly from God by infusion and not by human experience.

Another argument for Jesus' infused knowledge is given by St. Thomas. He points out, on the basis of his theory of knowledge borrowed from Aristotle, that the human mind, as spirit, has the capacity to know all created things – there is no limit to what the human mind can know. Lack of knowledge is considered an imperfection, and actual knowledge a perfection of the mind. Thomas argues that the union of Jesus' soul with the Word of God and his mission as Redeemer and Revealer require that he have the perfection of all possible human knowledge. Therefore, he argues, Jesus' soul possessed the fullness of divinely infused knowledge from the first moment of his conception.

What about acquired or experiential knowledge? Did Jesus have that kind of knowledge too? By "acquired knowledge" is meant the human knowledge which proceeds from the unique combination of sense perception with the abstracting activity of the intellect which produces concepts or universal ideas. Since it is a defined dogma of the Church that Jesus was fully human – possessing both body and soul – it follows necessarily that he had human-acquired or experiential knowledge. As St. Thomas remarked long ago, the denial of experiential knowledge in Christ leads eventually to the heresy of Docetism, that is, the theory that Jesus was not really a human being but merely "appeared" to be such.

The Gospels give many indications that Jesus made progress in human knowledge. In fact, St. Luke says in 2:52 that "Jesus increased in wisdom and in stature, and in favor with God and with man." In what sense did he make progress in human knowledge? It was not possible for him to "progress" in the immediate vision of God or in his infused knowledge since both of these types of knowledge, from the very beginning, encompassed all real things of the past, present, and future, as we have seen. With regard to these two types of knowledge, we can speak of "progress" only in the sense of a gradual manifestation that corresponded to the various stages of his physical growth. Thus, Jesus did not speak like an adult when he was a child, except perhaps on rare occasions. For example, his wisdom shone through at the age of twelve in the Temple when he replied to his Mother, "Did you not know that I must be in my Father's house?" (Luke 2:49).

That Jesus had acquired knowledge and that he made progress in human knowledge, we know from Scripture. *How* this was possible is another matter. There have been many theories to explain it; none of them is fully satisfactory. St. Thomas said that Jesus made progress in his human knowledge because he learned by experience what he already knew through his infused knowledge. Thus, he said that it was new, not in its content, but only in the way in which Christ acquired it. You may or may not find that explanation satisfactory. I have studied many of the modern theories, some quite different from that of St. Thomas, but I have not found one that is better.

In any event, to be in tune with the thinking of the Church, it is best, in my view, to hold that Jesus possessed both infused knowledge and acquired or experiential knowledge. We can leave the more subtle explanations to the theologians.

Chapter 6
The Powers of Jesus

We have seen that Jesus possessed, during his earthly life, the fullness of wisdom and knowledge. The next step in our consideration of Jesus Christ is to examine his will. It is by our will that we adhere to God or separate ourselves from him. Sin, or rebellion against God, resides in the will.

With this in mind we can ask at this point: Did Jesus ever sin? Was he capable of sinning? To those questions most Catholics would reply instinctively "No." That answer is perfectly correct. In the next place I would like to show why that answer is correct.

The New Testament attests in many places to the absolute sinlessness of Jesus Christ. "He committed no sin; no guile was found on his lips" (1 Pet. 2:22). "For we have not a high priest who is unable to sympathize with our weaknesses, but one who in every respect has been tempted as we are, yet without sin" (Heb. 4:15). And Jesus himself challenged his enemies: "Which of you convicts me of sin?" (John 8:46).

Various General Councils of the Church have declared that Jesus was free of all sin. The Council of Chalcedon in 451 said that he is "like us in every respect except sin"; here the Fathers quote Hebrews 4:15 cited above. In the further explanation of Jesus' sinlessness the Fathers and theologians deduce Christ's freedom from original sin from the Hypostatic Union – that totally mysterious union of the human nature and the divine nature in the Person of the Word. This most intimate connection with God excludes the condition of separation from God, which is the result of original sin.

According to Luke 1:35 Jesus entered into this world in a state of holiness: "The child to be born will be called holy, the Son of God." The Council of Trent defined that original sin is transmitted from one generation to the next by natural generation. Since Jesus Christ entered into this world in a supernatural way because of his conception by the Holy Spirit (Matt. 1:18ff.; Luke 1:20ff.), it follows that he was not subject to the general law for the transmission of original sin.

The sad consequences of original sin are our inclinations toward sin, our unruly passions, our difficulty in controlling ourselves, even when we seriously want to obey God. This inclination is called "concupiscence" in theological tradition. Trent also defined that concupiscence flows from original sin; it comes from sin, and it leads us into sin, but it itself is not sin. Thus, where there is no original sin there is no concupiscence. This is one of the aspects of Mary's Immaculate Conception. She was conceived without original sin, so she was not burdened with concupiscence and never committed any sin, not even a venial sin. Since Christ was also conceived without original sin, he was free from concupiscence. Thus, his sensual nature and his passions were completely subject to the direction of reason. Accordingly, the Fifth Council of Constantinople officially rejected the false teaching of some theologians that Christ "was burdened with the passions of the soul and with the desires of the flesh."[1]

1   DS 434; TCF 621.

So it is a defined dogma of the faith that Jesus never committed a sin. But was Jesus capable of sinning? Although it is not defined, it is a matter of Catholic faith that Jesus in his humanity was not merely sinless, but also that he was impeccable, that is, incapable of sinning. There are indications of this in the New Testament, some of which were cited above. The Bible, however, says that there was no sin in Jesus, but it does not say explicitly that he was *incapable* of sinning.

The Fifth Council of Constantinople (553) condemned a certain teaching which maintained that Christ became completely impeccable only after the Resurrection.[2] We may conclude from this that he was already impeccable before his death and Resurrection.

The basic reason for Jesus' impeccability is found again in the mysterious Hypostatic Union. What this means in practice is that the human acts of Jesus are the acts of the Second Person of the Blessed Trinity. Clearly, it is a contradiction to the absolute sanctity of God – the source of all sanctity – that a divine Person should be the responsible subject of a sinful act. Also, because of the Hypostatic Union, Christ's human will was totally penetrated and controlled by the divine will.

When it comes to explaining *how* Jesus' impeccability was brought about, the theologians are divided. The followers of St. Thomas teach that it was accomplished by the Beatific Vision possessed by Jesus from the first moment of his conception. In this view, the Beatific Vision by itself always renders sin absolutely impossible. For one who sees God as he is in himself cannot turn away from him in sin. For this reason, the blessed saints

2   DS 434; TCF 621.

in heaven can never sin and be cast out of the presence of
God.

Jesus and the fullness of grace

The goal of human life is personal union with God for all
eternity in knowledge and love. Union with God is called
sanctity or holiness, for God is the essence of holiness.
Thus, the closer one is to God, the holier one is.

As we have seen, our Lord Jesus Christ is both God
and man. Because of the Hypostatic Union Christ's
human nature is said to be substantially holy. The reason
for this is that the Word of God, who is uncreated holiness
itself, imparts a special holiness to his own created human
nature. Since the relationship between Jesus' human
nature and the Word of God is in the substantial order by
virtue of the Hypostatic Union, then it is legitimate to say
that his humanity is endowed with substantial sanctity or
holiness. For it is impossible to have a more intimate
union between a creature and God than the Hypostatic
Union in Jesus Christ. A suggestion of Jesus' substantial
holiness is given in Luke 1:35, "Therefore the child to be
born will be called holy, the Son of God."

In addition to the special "grace of union," as the above
is called, Christ's soul is also holy by reason of the fullness
of sanctifying grace with which it is endowed. By "sanctifying grace" here is meant the created habitual grace that
inheres in the soul of the justified. Jesus possesses the fullness of that grace. Thus, Pope Pius XII said in his encyclical letter of the Mystical Body in 1943: "In Him [Christ]
dwells the Holy Spirit with such a fullness of grace that
greater cannot be conceived." Basing their opinion on the

Gospel of St. John, all theologians ascribe sanctifying grace in its fullness to the human soul of Christ. "And the Word became flesh and dwelt among us, full of grace and truth. . . . And from his fullness have we all received, grace upon grace" (John 1:14, 16). In Acts 10:38 we read that "God anointed Jesus of Nazareth with the Holy Spirit"; in St. Luke we find that Jesus was "full of the Holy Spirit" (4:1); he also quoted Isaiah and said, "The Spirit of the Lord is upon me, because he has anointed me" (4:18).

St. Thomas Aquinas bases the sanctification of Jesus, humanity through sanctifying grace on three facts: 1) on the Hypostatic Union which demands the fullness of grace in Christ's soul according to the principle, "The nearer an effect is to its cause, the more in partakes of its influence"; 2) on the nobility of Christ's soul which enjoys the immediate vision of God; 3) on the relationship of Christ to all men since he is the Head and source of their grace.[3]

Because Christ possesses the fullness of all grace, he is able to bestow it on all the members of his Mystical Body, past, present, and future. In his wisdom and divine plan, God the Father has seen fit to dispense all grace to men through his only-begotten Son, Jesus Christ. Thus, all grace is the grace of Christ; all grace comes to us from and through him. In this regard, Pius XII said in the Letter quoted above: "From Him there flows out into the body of the Church all light through which the faithful receive supernatural enlightenment, and every grace, through which they become holy, as He Himself is holy. . . . Christ is the founder and originator of holiness. . . . Grace and glory well up from His inexhaustible fullness."

3 *Summa Theologiae* III, q. 7, art. 1.

With regard to the same point, St. John says: "And from his fullness have all received, grace upon grace" (1:16). St. Paul says that Christ as man is Head of the Church, which is his Mystical Body: "He has put all things under his foot and has made him the head over all things for the church, which is his body" (Eph. 1:22–23). Just as among human beings the life and control of the body are thought to be located in the head, so also the supernatural life of grace – in the spiritual order – flows from Christ the Head to the members of his Mystical Body. As God, Christ is the author and source of grace; through his human nature, as the instrument of the divinity, he confers grace upon individual persons through the Church and the sacraments.

The activity of Christ in bestowing grace extends to all men of all times, to the actual members who are united to him through sanctifying grace; to those who have faith; and to the potential members who do not yet have either faith or sanctifying grace. The only ones excluded from his grace are the damned in hell. The reason for the exclusion is that, since they have freely rejected God and his grace, they no longer have the capacity to receive grace.

It is very helpful to recall from time to time that our grace and salvation come from Jesus Christ and only from him (see Acts 4:12). Without him there is no grace and no salvation.

The power of Jesus

The next point to consider is the *power* of Jesus' humanity. In the Gospels, which are true historical records, we read about the many marvelous and miraculous things that Jesus did.

Here I would like to mention just a few of them. Jesus performed many miraculous cures of the sick and infirm – by the touch of his hand or by a mere word. St. Luke says in 6:19 about the crowds that followed him, "And all the crowd sought to touch him, for power came forth from him and healed them all." Even during his earthly life Jesus had power over nature and the powers of nature – over the power of gravity, over the fish, over the wind and the waves. St. Matthew related in 14:25–26, "And in the fourth watch of the night he came to them, walking on the sea. But when the disciples saw him walking on the sea, they were terrified."

In addition to his power over nature he also had power over the spiritual realities that concern man's relationship with almighty God. Thus, Jesus attributed to himself as the Son of man the power to forgive sins: "The Son of man has authority on earth to forgive sins" (Matt. 9:6). "He who eats my flesh and drinks my blood abides in me, and I in him. . . . He who eats this bread will live for ever" (John 6:56–58). In his prayer as High Priest before his passion Jesus confesses that the Father has given him power over "all flesh" or all mankind: "Father . . . the hour has come; glorify thy Son that the Son may glorify thee, since thou hast given him power over all flesh, to give eternal life to all whom thou hast given him" (John 17:2).

We know from our many years of reading the Scriptures, from hearing them read each Sunday at Mass, and from our study of the catechism that Jesus possessed extraordinary powers and that he performed many miracles. How did he do that? Did his human soul and body possess the omnipotent power of God so that he could do such remarkable things?

In order to get a clear picture of this mysterious reality, it is important to remember that God confers certain powers on the nature of things he has created. Occasionally, for a spiritual purpose, he goes beyond the normal powers of nature; that is what we mean by a "miracle." Christ's human nature was endowed with certain powers of nature and grace, but those powers were finite, not infinite. Jesus as man was not omnipotent. In his human nature, which was created and finite, Jesus was not omnipotent. Omnipotence is a perfection which pertains to the divinity alone.

But with regard to producing supernatural effects, such as miracles, prophecies, and the forgiveness of sins, Jesus' human nature functions as an instrument of the Word. So he has instrumental power to produce supernatural effects in the physical order which serve the purpose of redemption, that is, the salvation of mankind.

The key here to understanding Jesus' supernatural power is the Hypostatic Union, which has been referred to many times in this study. This means that the human nature of Jesus is substantially united to the Second Person of the Blessed Trinity – the infinite, divine Word of God. The principal cause of the miraculous and supernatural effects produced by Jesus is therefore the Word of God who operates in and through the humanity of Jesus which is his own. There is a certain similarity here to the painter who uses a brush to paint a beautiful picture. The painter is the principal cause of the picture, but he uses the brush as an instrument. The efficient cause of the picture is the creative power of the artist, although the brush also contributes something. Likewise, the divine power operates in and through Jesus Christ, but the principal cause is the divine power of the Word while the humanity functions as the instrumental cause.

The Fathers of the Church understood the humanity of Christ to be an instrument of the Godhead. Therefore, they said that the flesh of Christ has the power to give life. St. Cyril of Alexandria said of the Eucharist which is the Body and Blood of Christ: "As the flesh of the Redeemer, through His union with substantial life, that is, with the Word stemming from God, is become life-giving, we, when we enjoy it, have life in us."[4]

The point of this consideration is to realize that Jesus possesses divine power to produce effects in the order of nature that surpass the powers of nature, and to produce effects in the order of divine grace that pertain to God alone. Jesus, however, who is both God and man, possesses infinite power because he is God, not because he is man. Thus, Christ's humanity, as instrument of the divine Word, produces and can produce supernatural effects through the power received from God.

Jesus Christ is the Head of the Church which is his Mystical Body. The glorified Christ in heaven continues to pour out his Spirit on the faithful. He showers his grace on us through his sacraments, especially through the reception of his Body and Blood in the Eucharist.

Jesus' human feelings and limitations

Having considered Jesus' perfections in the areas of knowledge, sanctity, and power, the next point to

4   DS 262; TCF 606/11.

consider is the question of the defects or limitations he labored under in both body and soul. By "defects" in this context I do not mean moral faults, but merely certain aspects of the human condition as the result of which we are able to suffer either in the body or in the soul.

The questions I hope to answer are the following: Did Jesus really suffer pain in his body as we do? Also, did Jesus endure mental suffering such as we are exposed to, for example, sadness and fear? We ask these questions because, now aware of his infinite dignity by reason of the Hypostatic Union, we might be led to think that he did not suffer under the same weaknesses and defects that we do.

There were some heretics in the early Church, called "Docetists," who said that Jesus did not have a human body and soul like ours and that therefore he could not suffer as we do. The Church reacted strongly against this error and repeatedly condemned it. For, if that were true, then Jesus would not truly be one of us – be our Brother; it would mean that he did not really suffer and die for our salvation; it would in effect mean the end of the Church and the sacraments.

Against that heretical view the Church in her Creed professes that Jesus really suffered and died under Pontius Pilate. The Fourth Lateran Council in the year 1215 declared that Jesus "in His humanity was made capable of suffering and death."[5] Thus, it is the defined teaching of the Catholic Church that Jesus could and did suffer pains just as we do. The fact that he was God – the Second Person of the Blessed Trinity incarnate – did not prevent him from suffering and dying as we do.

5   DS 801; TCF 20.

Since Jesus was free from all sin, however, including original sin, his bodily defects and limitations were not the consequence of sin as they are for us. The defects we are talking about are hunger, thirst, weariness, feeling of pain, and mortality. Jesus voluntarily assumed these common human weaknesses for three reasons: 1) to satisfy for the sins of mankind by undergoing the punishment due to sin, such as fatigue, pain, and death; 2) to confirm the faith of mankind in the truth of the Incarnation, that is, that he truly is a human being as we are; 3) to give Christians an example of those virtues of patience and endurance that they ought to imitate in their own lives.

It would not be correct to say that these defects were unnatural in Christ because he is God. They were natural because they belong to human nature as such in its present condition. The point is that he *freely* assumed them. Because he was God incarnate he could have assumed a human nature without them.

We might note, though, that Jesus' work of redemption required only that he assume the general human defects as such, i.e., hunger, thirst, fatigue, pain, and death. He did not assume particular defects that often are the result of moral faults, like illness of body or soul, or that are opposed to the perfection of the soul, like ignorance.

At this point I would ask you to recall that Jesus, already in his earthly life, possessed the immediate vision of God plus infused knowledge of all things past, present, and future. Consequently, he was absolutely free of all ignorance and error. This situation suggests a question about Jesus' emotions and feelings. Our passions and emotions often induce us to do or say things (for example, in a fit of anger) that are contrary to reason and that we later regret. So did Jesus have emotions? Did he experience the push and pull of feelings as we do?

For those familiar with the four Gospels the answer is clear: Yes, Jesus was subject to emotions. We find various emotions explicitly attributed to him in the Gospels. "He began to be *sorrowful* and *troubled*" (Matt. 26:37). "He began to be greatly *distressed* and *troubled*" (Mark 14:33). "And he looked around at them with *anger*" (Mark 3:5). "For your sake I am *glad*" (John 11:15).

It is not surprising that it should be so since Jesus was fully human, just as we are, except for sin. What happens to the body affects the soul, and vice versa, because man is one composite being. That is the whole point in contemporary psychosomatic medicine. We have already shown that Jesus suffered bodily ills; it follows, then, that he also felt human emotions like sadness and joy.

Because of Jesus' freedom from concupiscence, however, his passions and emotions could not be directed to a sinful object, could not even arise in him without his consent – they were completely under the control of his will and could not obscure or dominate his mind. In this regard there is a significant difference between his emotions and ours. For, our emotions arise spontaneously, often against our will, and sometimes totally dominate our power of reason. Thus, they can lead us into sin. Not so with Jesus. Jesus was capable of suffering and experienced emotions, but everything was under the control of his will which was totally obedient to his Father.

Chapter 7
Jesus Our Savior

We have been considering the Person of our Redeemer, the Lord Jesus Christ. Now we will reflect on what it is he came to do in this world, that is, the work of our redemption or salvation.

We sometimes speak about Jesus as "our dear Savior" – and indeed he is. Even a short reflection on the Incarnation – the implications of the Hypostatic Union – necessarily lead one to ask in a state of wonder: "Why did God do it?" "Why did God humble himself to such an extent that he actually assumed our weak human flesh?"

The Bible and the Church, which alone can authentically interpret the Bible, say clearly that the Son of God – the Second Person of the Blessed Trinity – became man in order to redeem mankind. In other words, the *purpose* of the Incarnation was our redemption from sin.

We are familiar with the idea from the Creed that we profess at Mass each Sunday: "I believe in one Lord, Jesus Christ. . . . For us men and for our salvation he came down from heaven."

The New Testament says often that Christ came into the world to save all men, to redeem them from their sins. The very name of "Jesus," which means "Savior," affirms his redemptive mission. Thus, we read in Matthew 1:21, "You shall call his name Jesus, for he will save his people from their sins." Speaking of himself and his work, Jesus said: "For the Son of man came to seek and to save the lost" (Luke 19:10). In Matthew 20:28 he said something quite similar: "The Son of man came not to be served but to serve, and to give his life as a ransom for many."

We find the same idea in St. John's Gospel: "For God sent the Son into the world, not to condemn the world, but that the world might be saved through him" (3:17).

St. Paul is probably the most outspoken writer in the New Testament about the redemptive purpose of the Incarnation. "When the time had fully come, God sent forth his Son, born of a woman, born under the law, to redeem those who were born under the law, so that we might receive adoption as sons" (Gal. 4:4). Again, Paul says very clearly in 1Timothy 1:15, "The saying is sure and worthy of full acceptance, that Christ Jesus came into the world to save sinners."

Everything God does outside himself is for his own glory in one way or another. Thus, the New Testament mentions another purpose of the Incarnation. It is the Glory of God which is the ultimate purpose of all God's works. Thus, the angels sing at Bethlehem, "Glory to God in the highest" (Luke 2:14). And before he goes to his death Jesus prays, "I glorified thee on earth, having accomplished the work which thou gavest me to do" (John 17:4).

For many centuries there has been a controversy among Catholic theologians about God's *primary* purpose in becoming man. Most, following St. Thomas Aquinas, say that the primary purpose was the redemption of mankind from sin. They conclude from this position that, if Adam and Eve had not sinned and so transmitted original sin to all their descendants, the Incarnation would not have taken place. Other theologians, following the Franciscan, Duns Scotus, maintain that the primary purpose of the Incarnation was the primacy of Jesus Christ over all creation – angels, world, and men. They say that the Son of God, in order to crown the work of creation, would have become man even without the fall of original sin.

The testimony of the New Testament favors the view of St. Thomas, as is clear from the citations given above.[1] There are many texts in the New Testament which say explicitly that the purpose of the Incarnation was the redemption of mankind. On the other hand, there is not one text in the New Testament which says that the Incarnation would have taken place even without the Fall of our first parents.

The Fathers of the Church are practically unanimous in the same opinion. St. Augustine said: "If mankind had not fallen, the Son of Man would not have come. . . . Why did He come into the world? To save sinners [1 Tim. 1:15]. There is no other reason given in Scripture for his coming into the world."

The Incarnation is God's most sublime work. The followers of Scotus find it inappropriate that sin, which God hates, should be the occasion for the greatest revelation of God. The Thomists see in that an even greater proof of God's infinite love and mercy.

The Scotists seek the biblical proof for their view in the teaching of St. Paul that creation is ordered to Christ as to its head and crown. The main text they use is Colossians 1:15–20, where Christ is said to be "the first-

---

1   *Summa Theologiae* III, q. 1, art. 3).

born of all creation" (v. 15). Also, "in him all things were created" (v. 16). Also, "He is the beginning, the first-born from the dead, that in everything he might be pre-eminent" (v. 18). The Thomists reply that these texts prescind from the Incarnation and refer to the Second Person of the Blessed Trinity, who is the eternal and infinite God.

The view of St. Thomas on the primary purpose of the Incarnation is not as lofty and all-encompassing as that of Scotus, but it is more in accord with the data of revelation, that is, what God told us about himself.

The view of St. Thomas is to be preferred because we are not in a position to say what God would have done if Adam and Eve had not sinned. He did not reveal that to us. Many statements in the New Testament can be summed up in the following proposition: "Christ Jesus came into the world to save sinners."

Jesus Christ is the Redeemer of mankind

Christ came into this world to redeem us, so one of the common titles we give to Jesus is that he is our "Redeemer." What does the Church mean by the word "redemption"?

In ordinary usage we say that one can "redeem" something, such as a coat or a suitcase, by making a payment or by presenting a ticket that one has paid for in advance. The idea is related to what is meant by the word "ransom." We use this word in reference to a payment made to a kidnapper for the release of the person or thing taken and held.

Both of these ideas have been used by theologians to explain what is meant by the redemption of mankind by

Jesus Christ, the God-man. Other ideas used to explain it include liberation and deliverance. Jesus is the Great Liberator who frees us from our sins and restores us to friendship with Almighty God, who was offended by the sin of Adam and by our own personal sins.

The term "redemption" in Christian theology, therefore, refers to the mystery of God's deliverance of mankind from the evil of sin and his restoration of man to the state of grace and friendship with God by an act of divine power and merciful love. God's redemptive act in Jesus Christ includes the whole of man's history from the time of his first sin and fall from grace, as St. Paul intimates in 1 Timothy 2:4, "God our Savior . . . desires all men to be saved, and to come to the knowledge of the truth."

There are two ways of looking at the work of redemption. First, we can consider it as the work done on our behalf by the God-man, Jesus Christ. In this sense it includes the Incarnation of the Second Person of the Blessed Trinity, the life, passion, death and Resurrection of Jesus. His work of redemption brought about the salvation of mankind from the slavery of sin, which includes separation from God, suffering, death, and subjection to the power of the devil. St. Paul expresses this idea clearly in Romans 3:23–24: "Since all have sinned and fall short of the glory of God, they are justified by his grace as a gift, through the redemption which is in Christ Jesus, whom God put forward as an expiation by his blood, to be received by faith."

Second, we can consider the redemption as the application of the grace of Jesus Christ to individual men and women. Thus, those who believe in Jesus Christ, repent of their sins, and are baptized into the community of the faithful receive the grace of Christ, which makes them children of God and heirs of heaven.

Redemption is directed against sin and its power over the soul. Its purpose is to liberate us from sin and the power of the devil. By its very nature sin is a turning away from God and a turning toward creatures. The work of redemption, therefore, must consist in turning men away from a disordered attachment to creatures and turning them toward God. On this point St. Paul says that the heavenly Father "has delivered us from the dominion of darkness and transferred us to the kingdom of his beloved Son, in whom we have redemption, the forgiveness of sins" (Col. 1:13–14).

Our redemption, objectively considered, was accomplished by the teaching, life, death, and Resurrection of Jesus Christ. In a very special way, however, it was effected by the vicarious atonement of the merits of Christ in his sacrificial death on the Cross. Through the atonement the offense offered to God by sin was counterbalanced and the injury to the honor of God was repaired. By his death Christ merited a superabundance of grace, which is dispensed to all men of all times to bring about their redemption.

Because the offense of sin is against the infinite dignity of God, and because man – as a creature – is totally dependent on God, he is not able to save himself. Thus, he needs assistance from God; he needs a mediator who can reconcile him with God.

Jesus Christ was able to redeem mankind because he is both God and man, and therefore his actions and merits have infinite value and so can make adequate reparation for the sins committed against God. He is a divine Person – the Second Person of the Blessed Trinity –

substantially united to a human nature. In virtue of his divine-human constitution Jesus is the Mediator between God and mankind, as Paul says in 1 Timothy 2:5, "For there is one God, and there is one mediator between God and men, the man Christ Jesus, who gave himself as a ransom for all."

In the order of being and activity the God-man Jesus Christ is the only Mediator between God and man. Other mediators, such as the angels and saints, are all subordinated to the mediation of Christ. Jesus Christ mediated and mediates for us through the actions of his human nature. Because of the real distinction between his two natures – divine and human – it was possible for him to perform mediatory acts as man and receive them as God. This answers the objection that Christ could not act as mediator between himself (as God) and mankind.

Fallen man needs a Redeemer

Jesus Christ has liberated us from both original sin and our own personal sins. In order to stir up sentiments of gratitude to God for such a Redeemer, it might be helpful to reflect here for a few moments on the necessity and freedom of our redemption.

Given Adam's sin, which was passed on to all his descendants and which is open rebellion against God the Creator, and our own personal sins, what can man do when he comes to the realization of his own evil and wishes to be reconciled with his Creator and God? The Church answers: By his own efforts man can do nothing to save himself, to redeem himself, to regain the lost friendship with God. Here is what the Council of Trent had to say on this point:

> It is necessary to admit that all men had lost inno-
> cence in the sin of Adam. They became unclean.
> . . . They "were by nature children of wrath" (Eph
> 2:3). . . . So completely were they slaves of sin and
> under the power of the devil and death, that nei-
> ther the power of nature for the Gentiles nor the
> very letter of the Law of Moses for the Jews could
> bring liberation from that condition.[2]

In other words, the Catholic Church teaches infallibly that fallen man, namely all of us, cannot redeem himself. If he is to attain his final end in the face-to-face vision of God, he is in desperate need of God's help. Just as all are under the curse of sin, so also all need the grace of Jesus Christ.

Jesus Christ is the second Adam – the beginning of a new people of God. Just as the first Adam lost for himself and for us the grace of God, so the second Adam, by his sacrificial suffering and death, regained for us what the first Adam had lost. It is essential to note that sanctifying grace, which makes man a friend of God, is wholly supernatural. That means that it is a free personal gift of God over and above the first gift of natural existence. In theological terms, this means that God could have creat-ed man in a purely natural state, with a natural end, without ordaining him to the Beatific Vision in the next life. But to the first gift of nature, because of his divine love and goodness, he added the second gift of sanctify-ing grace which is wholly supernatural and not required by the first gift.

2   DS 1521; TCF 1925.

Because of his infinite love and mercy, God came into our world of time and space and assumed a human nature in order to restore the supernatural gift of sancti-fying grace that had been lost for us by the first Adam. This is what we mean by "redemption," and this is some-thing that man could not accomplish by his own natural powers.

In trying to understand our redemption it helps also to consider the nature of sin. Sin is rebellion, a personal offense against God our Creator, and a violation of his will and his law. Man is a finite, limited creature; God is infinite goodness and perfection. Personal offenses are measured not only by what is done, but also by the dig-nity of the person offended. Thus, an insulting word offered by one child to another is not as serious as the same insulting word uttered by a son to his father. Likewise, the offense of one man against another is not the same as an offense of a man against God. For, the dig-nity of God infinitely surpasses the dignity of the human person.

Thus, the basic reason for the absolute necessity of redemption for fallen man is found both in the supernat-uralness of sanctifying grace and the infinity, in one sense, of man's guilt that is found in sin. As an action of a creature, sin is certainly finite; but if we consider sin as an insult to the infinite God – which it is – then it is infi-nite. It should be obvious that an infinite offense requires infinite satisfaction or atonement. Man is not capable of that because he is utterly finite. Therefore, only God can make adequate satisfaction to himself – only a divine Person can do that.

We Catholics believe – and we profess in our Creed – that the Son of God became man to redeem us and to save us from the power of Satan, sin, and death. Was God under any compulsion to redeem us? No. Our redemption was a perfectly free act of divine love and mercy.

Another question that occurs is this: On the supposition that God resolved to redeem man, was the Incarnation of the Second Person of the Blessed Trinity absolutely necessary to accomplish this? St. Thomas Aquinas asked this question and replied that God, because of his omnipotence, could have redeemed mankind in many other ways. It would be an unwarranted limitation on his power and mercy to say that the Incarnation was his only means of redeeming us. Without injury to his justice, God can grant forgiveness to the repentant sinner even without adequate satisfaction.

The Incarnation of the Word, the Second Person of the Trinity, however, was most fitting. It was the most appropriate means of redeeming us because it reveals the perfections of God in a most glorious manner and also offers the strongest motives and best example to men and women to strive for religious and moral perfection by imitating Jesus Christ, the incarnate God.

Jesus, the Divine Teacher

By his death and resurrection Jesus triumphed over the powers of Satan, sin, and death. He actually accomplished our redemption through his three offices or functions, which are traditionally called the prophetic office, pastoral or kingly office, and priestly office. Thus, in many official Church documents reference is made to our Lord as prophet, pastor or king, and priest. For example, the Second Vatican Council in its Constitution on the

Church speaks explicitly about these three offices of Jesus Christ. They are indicated also in John 14:6, "I am the way [pastor], the truth [teacher] and the life [priest]."

We will next consider a few aspects of Jesus' prophetic or teaching office. Certainly, we get our best picture of the Lord Jesus in the four Gospels, and there he is frequently presented as a teacher of the truth. We see him teaching his disciples, instructing the people. One of the most memorable passages in the New Testament is the Sermon on the Mount in Matthew, chapters five to seven. There Jesus is presented as a second Moses, teaching the people about God and the way to God.

A consequence of original sin, ratified by personal sin, is that man is caught up in religious ignorance. This ignorance came into the world through the deception of the devil, who is "a liar and the father of lies" (John 8:44). The Redeemer came into the world "to destroy the works of the devil" (1 John 3:8) and to free mankind from his slavery, a part of which is both ignorance about God and false ideas about God's nature and existence. An essential part of this task was to remove man's spiritual darkness, which is the result of sin, and to bring the bright light of true knowledge about God. Hence, one of Jesus' major tasks as our Redeemer was to instruct us about the nature of God and about his divine plan for the salvation of mankind.

Truth of itself possesses tremendous liberating power. Jesus proclaimed the redeeming power of truth when he said, "You will know the truth, and the truth will make you free" (John 8:32). Jesus both speaks the truth and is the truth.

Some readers may not immediately perceive the connection between "teacher" and "prophet." In biblical terms, the prophet is simply one who speaks in the name of God, whether to express his demands or his promises for the future. He proclaims to the people what God's will is for them and what he expects them to do. Predicting the future – a notion usually associated with prophecy – is only one aspect of the prophetic office. But since God's plan for the world will be fully realized only in the future, when the prophets advert to that there is always an element of prediction in their prophecies.

The Jews of Jesus' time were expecting another great prophet. For Moses had said in Deuteronomy 18:15, "The Lord your God will raise up for you a prophet like me from among you, from your brethren – him you shall heed." The New Testament authors refer this text to Jesus (see Acts 3:22; 7:37; John 1:45). So Jesus is often spoken of as a prophet.

Jesus calls himself "the light of the world" (John 8:12), "the truth," and considers the proclamation of the truth as one of his principal tasks: "For this I was born, and for this I have come into the world, to bear witness to the truth. Every one who is of the truth hears my voice" (John 18:37).

Jesus is also often called "Rabbi," which means "teacher," and he claims to be the only teacher of man: "Neither be called masters, for you have one master, the Christ" (Matt. 23:10). So Jesus is the teacher of mankind. His teaching, of course, does not concern human affairs and human science. Jesus is exclusively concerned about God and man, and man's way to God.

There is no doubt that Jesus' teaching made a powerful impact on his listeners. The Gospels often use the word "amazement" to describe the reactions of his audience. When the police sent to arrest Jesus returned empty-handed, they said to their angry superiors, "No man ever spoke like this man!" (John 7:46). At the conclusion of the Sermon on the Mount, Matthew says, "When Jesus finished these sayings, the crowds were astonished at his teaching, for he taught them as one who had authority, and not as their scribes" (7:28–29).

The foundation of Jesus' unique teaching authority lies, again, in the mysterious Hypostatic Union – one divine Person subsisting in two natures – the divine nature and the human nature. In virtue of that union, as we have seen, he possesses the immediate vision of God and infused knowledge of all things past, present and future. Because of that knowledge he is "the Truth" and speaks the truth with absolute confidence and authority. Jesus gave his right to teach all men to his Apostles and their successors: "All authority in heaven and on earth has been given to me. Go therefore and make disciples of all nations, baptizing them in the name of the Father and of the Son and of the Holy Spirit, teaching them to observe all that I have commanded you; and lo, I am with you always to the close of the age" (Matt. 28:18–20).

King of Kings, and Lord of Lords

Jesus Christ is king, there is no doubt about that. In reply to Pontius Pilate who asked Jesus if he was a king, he said, "Yes, I am a king" (John 18:37). It is perhaps difficult for Americans to grasp easily what a king is, since we have experienced over two hundred years of democratic government. Our ancestors declared independence from the English King because of certain grievances that were not redressed.

We might ask ourselves: What is a king? The Webster's Dictionary defines it thus: "a male monarch of a major territorial unit; esp.: one who inherits his position and rules for life." An absolute monarch, like Louis XIV of France, incorporates in his own person all three functions of normal government – legislative, judicial, and executive. Various limits can and have been put on kings and their heirs. There are current examples of this in constitutional monarchies such as England, Belgium, and Spain. In the course of history kings in those countries have been stripped of most of their powers so that their function has become ceremonial for the most part.

We know from the New Testament that Jesus Christ is a king – he said so himself. Jesus is also the shepherd or pastor of his flock, that is, all those who believe in him and follow him. In church language the words "king" and "pastor," when applied to Jesus, have more or less the same meaning. They refer to his power or authority to rule over the people of God. Just as a shepherd or pastor rules over his flock of sheep, and just as an earthly king rules over the people in his territory, so also Jesus Christ, King of Kings and Lord of Lords, rules over his Church. Accordingly, Christ's pastoral or kingly office manifests itself in legislation, in judicial functions and in the execution of his judgments.

The Old Testament prophecies proclaimed a great messianic king who would be sent to redeem God's people (see Ps. 2; Isa. 9:6ff.; Dan. 7:13ff.). The New Testament says that those prophecies have been fulfilled in Jesus of Nazareth. Thus, the angel Gabriel said to Mary at the Annunciation: "The Lord God will give to him the throne of his father David, and he will reign over the house of Jacob forever" (Luke 1:32). Before Pontius Pilate, the

Roman governor, Jesus openly proclaimed himself to be a king. At the same time, however, he made it clear that his kingdom is spiritual and not of this world: "My kingship is not of this world" (John 18:36). Before his Ascension into heaven, when he gave his great commission to his Apostles, Jesus stated that his royal power embraces both heaven and earth: "All authority in heaven and on earth has been given to me" (Matt. 28:18).

Jesus confirmed his legislative or lawgiving power when he promulgated the basic law of his kingdom in the Sermon on the Mount. He preached the arrival of the kingdom of God on earth and gave it visibility in his Church which was founded on Peter and the other Apostles (Matt. 16:18–19; 18:18). He established the new commandment of love for one another (John 13:34) and demanded strict observance of his commandments (John 14:15; Matt. 28:20).

Jesus also possessed supreme judicial power: "The Father judges no one, but has given all judgment to the Son" (John 5:22). We also pray in the ancient Apostles' Creed: "From thence he shall come to judge the living and the dead." So Jesus is the supreme and eternal judge of all men of all time. The judgment that the Son will hand down on the last day will be executed or carried out immediately: "And they [the evil ones] will go away into eternal punishment, but the righteous into eternal life" (Matt. 25:46).

Martin Luther said that Christ did not give any commands, but only promises. In opposition to that teaching the Council of Trent declared in the sixteenth century: "If anyone says that God has given Jesus Christ to men as a redeemer in whom they are to trust, but not as a lawgiver whom they are to obey: let him be anathema," that is, expelled from the Church community.[3] So Jesus is a law-giver – one of the functions of a ruling king.

Since the time of the early Fathers of the Church, Jesus has been addressed and adored as a king. Some saw him as a king ruling from the word of the Cross. In 1925 Pope Pius XI published a beautiful encyclical letter on the universal kingship of Christ, entitled *Quas Primas*. By the order of the same Holy Father the feast of Christ the King was instituted for the universal Church on the last Sunday of October. Since the liturgical reform by Pope Paul VI after Vatican II the feast is celebrated in the Ordinary Form of the Roman Rite on the last Sunday of the liturgical year in late November. In the Extraordinary Form of the Roman Rite it is celebrated on the last Sunday of October.

Jesus is a Priest forever

The third office attributed to Jesus by Holy Scripture is that of priest. The Old Testament text most often applied to Jesus in the New Testament is Psalm 110:4, which affirms his eternal priesthood: "You are a priest for ever after the order of Melchizedek."

In order to understand why Scripture and the Church affirm that the God-man Jesus Christ is a priest, it is necessary to have a clear idea of what a priest is. A basic notion of priesthood is "mediation" or "to be a mediator." A mediator is one who stands in the middle between two extremes; he is a go-between. Thus, when a child has a serious conflict with his father, he will often plead with

3   DS 1571; TCF 1971.

his mother to act as a "mediator" between himself and his father. The function of a mediator is to bring about a reconciliation between two opposed parties. Acceptable to both sides, he is able to facilitate communication back and forth and to work out an agreement or "reconciliation."

That is exactly what Jesus is – a mediator between God and men. Offended by the sin of Adam and by our own personal sins, God punished man with death and became inaccessible. In order to get back into God's good graces, man needed to be reconciled with him. Being finite and sinful, man needed a "bridge builder" or mediator who could establish contact with God and work out a settlement. That is where the God-man Jesus Christ came into the picture. St. Paul expresses this thought beautifully in 1Tim. 2:5–6, "For there is one God, and there is one mediator between God and men, the man Christ Jesus, who gave himself as a ransom for all."

Another essential notion involved with priesthood is that of "sacrifice." A priest is more than one who "ministers" to others by proclaiming to them God's Word, by teaching them and by leading them in prayer. That is the Protestant idea of a minister. The Catholic idea of the priesthood includes all that, but also adds the reality and function of "sacrifice." "Sacrifice" in this sense means to offer something precious and good to God, to remove it from our possession and place it in God's hands; the purpose of this act is to give external, visible expression to our internal, invisible obedience and subjection to his will.

Mediation between God and mankind is a two-way street. The priest offers gifts and sacrifices to God on behalf of mankind; he also brings gifts and blessings from God back to the human family. Thus, we read in Hebrews 5:1, "For every high priest chosen from among men is appointed to act on behalf of men in relation to God, to offer gifts and sacrifices for sins." In the Catholic faith and understanding, the priest brings God's gifts and graces to mankind by administering the holy sacraments, especially by offering the Holy Sacrifice of the Mass and by bringing Christ to the faithful in the Holy Eucharist as the food for their souls.

It is a truth of the Catholic faith that Jesus is a priest; in fact, the Bible and the Church documents refer to him as our "high priest," that is, principal, leading, or supreme priest. The Letter to the Hebrews offers us a whole treatise on Jesus' priesthood. For example, in 3:1we read, "Therefore, holy brethren, who share in a heavenly call, consider Jesus, the apostle and high priest of our confession." Basing themselves on this text and others like it, the bishops at the Council of Ephesus in 431 A.D. said, "If anyone, therefore, says that it was not the Word of God himself who was born to be our high priest and apostle when he was made flesh [see John 1:14] . . . let him be anathema."[4]

In 1562 the Council of Trent declared that the Levitical priesthood of the Old Testament was insufficient. Then the Council said: "It was, therefore, necessary (according to the merciful ordination of God the Father) that another priest arise according to the order of Melchizedek [see Gen. 14:18; Ps. 110:4; Heb. 7:11], our Lord Jesus Christ, who could perfect all who were to be sanctified [see Heb. 10:14] and bring them to fulfillment."[5]

4   DS 201; TCF 606/10.

What is it that constitutes Jesus as our mediator or high priest? It is the Hypostatic Union – the unique and eternal union of the divine nature and the human nature in the Person of the Word of God – which commenced at the moment of the Incarnation when the Virgin Mary consented to be the Mother of God. By reason of the Hypostatic Union Jesus Christ, because he is both God and man, stands, as it were, in the middle between God and man. Therefore, he can offer a sacrifice that is wholly pleasing to the Father and he can bring the grace of God to all mankind because he is our Brother. Finally, because the Hypostatic Union will last for all eternity, so also is Jesus our high priest forever.

5   DS 1739; TCF 1546.

Chapter 8
Jesus' Glorification

We have seen that Jesus is a priest forever. What I would next like to explain is the Church's belief and teaching that Jesus' bloody death on the Cross was a true *sacrifice.* We all have some idea of what a "sacrifice" is in the secular sense, that is, the giving up of some present good for the sake of something better. Thus, many parents deny themselves certain luxuries, such as a new car or a trip to Rome or a pleasure boat, in order to have the necessary money to send their children to college. Real accomplishment and perfection in any line of human endeavor, whether it be tennis, biology, or playing the piano, requires giving up or sacrificing other things, often much more pleasant, that one would like to do.

In the liturgical sense, such as we find in the Old Testament, a sacrifice is an external religious act in which a gift perceptible to the senses is offered to God by a specially designated person in recognition of his absolute sovereignty and in atonement for sins. Thus, we distinguish four elements in every true sacrifice: the person to whom it is offered, the one who offers, the visible gift, and the purpose for which the offering is made.

All of these elements are present in Jesus' death on the Cross. For Jesus himself is both the priest and the victim; he offered himself to the Father in atonement for the sins of all mankind.

The Council of Ephesus in 431 A.D. taught that Jesus offered himself up as a pleasing sacrifice to our God and Father. In formulating that teaching they relied on the words of St. Paul to the Ephesians found in 5:2, "Walk in love, as Christ loved us and gave himself up for us, a fragrant offering and sacrifice to God."

Some of the Fathers of the Church looked upon the Cross of Jesus as a type of altar of sacrifice. This idea was picked up and incorporated into the official teaching of the Church by the Council of Trent in 1562. In pointing out the relationship between Jesus' bloody sacrifice on the Cross and the Holy Mass, the Fathers said: "In the divine sacrifice that is offered in the Mass, the same Christ who offered himself once in a bloody manner *on the altar of the cross* is present and is offered in an unbloody manner."[1]

In the New Testament there are many references, both direct and indirect, to the sacrificial character of Jesus' death on Calvary. Thus, St. John the Baptist, following the prophet Isaiah, sees in Jesus the Lamb of sacrifice, who took on himself the sins of all mankind, in order to atone for them. Seeing Jesus approach the Jordan, St. John exclaimed to his followers: "Behold, the Lamb of God, who takes away the sin of the world" (John 1:29). St. Paul says of him in 1 Corinthians 5:7, "For Christ, our paschal lamb, has been sacrificed."

In the Gospels Jesus, on a number of occasions, speaks of "giving" his life for us. The Greek words used for these expressions are the same ones used in the Septuagint or Greek version of the Old Testament which was current at the time; in the Old Testament these words

1   DS 1743; TCF 1548.

are used in connection with the prescribed sacrifices that had to be offered at certain times of the year. For example, we read in Matthew 20:28, "The Son of man came not to be served but to serve, and to give his life as a ransom for many."

When he instituted the Holy Eucharist at the Last Supper, Jesus indicated the sacrificial nature of his death by the very words he used – words which are repeated by the Church each day in the Mass: "This is my body which is *given* for you" (Luke 22:19); "This is my blood of the covenant, which is *poured out* for many for the forgiveness of sins" (Matt. 26:28). In the context, the words "given" and "poured out" have a sacrificial meaning.

It should be clear, then, that Jesus' death on the Cross was a true sacrifice because it fulfilled all the requirements of a sacrificial act. As man, Jesus was at the same time both sacrificing priest and sacrificial gift. As God, together with the Father and the Holy Spirit, he was also the one who received the sacrifice.

The act of sacrifice consisted in the fact that Jesus, in an attitude of perfect self-surrender, voluntarily gave up his life to God by allowing his enemies to kill him, even though he could have prevented it. For he said in John 10:18, "No one takes it [my life] from me, but I lay it down of my own accord. I have power to lay it down, and I have power to take it again."

What does "Redemption" mean?

After considering Jesus' bloody death on Calvary as a true sacrifice, we are naturally led to ask, "Why did Jesus die?" or "What was the purpose of his violent and sacrificial death?" Questions such as these lead us naturally to the idea of "redemption" and "reconciliation" with God. Because Jesus is both God and man, all of his activities have redemptive value for us. Nevertheless, the culmination of his redemptive activity on our behalf is found in his sacrificial death on the Cross. For it was by his death, freely and lovingly embraced in obedience to the will of the Father, that Jesus accomplished our redemption.

The official teaching of the Church on this matter is that, by his sacrifice on the Cross, Jesus redeemed us and reconciled us with God. In 1562 the Council of Trent taught that Jesus offered himself to the Father on the altar of the Cross in order to accomplish for us "an everlasting redemption."[2]

This teaching, of course, is merely a repetition of a truth that is often stated in the New Testament. Thus, Jesus says in Matthew 20:28, "The Son of man came . . . to give his life as a ransom for many." And St. Paul says in Romans 5:8, "God shows his love for us in that while we were yet sinners Christ died for us." That Jesus redeemed us from our sins by his death is a recurring theme in the letters of St. Paul. "Since all have sinned and fall short of the glory of God, they are justified by his grace as a gift, through the redemption which is in Christ Jesus, whom God put forward as an expiation by his blood, to be received by faith" (Rom. 3:23–24).

Modern Americans often find it hard to understand clearly what is meant by the word "redemption." But it is both useful and important to grasp the idea involved in "redemption" since it is such a fundamental aspect of our Catholic faith. After all, two of the most common titles

2   DS 1740; TCF 1546.

attributed to our Lord refer to this mystery; they are "Redeemer" and "Savior."

The word "redemption" means the buying back, or ransoming, of a slave or captive in order to secure his freedom. In this sense it means almost the same thing as "liberation." The biblical use of "redemption" to signify the saving action of God with regard to his people has made it the term par excellence for expressing the meaning of the Cross of Christ.

What has Jesus saved us from? By his sacrificial death he has liberated us from the slavery of sin (Titus 2:14), death (2 Tim. 1:10), and the devil (Col. 1:13). Jesus asserts the atoning power of his death at the Last Supper: "For this is my blood of the covenant, which is poured out for many for the forgiveness of sins" (Matt. 26:28).

Sin is the big obstacle. Because of the sin of Adam and Eve, which is confirmed and repeated by the personal sins of mankind, a barrier was set up between man and God. Because of the sin of Adam, death and all the evils related to it entered into the world. As long as sin remained, there was enmity or hostility between man and his Creator. Jesus Christ came into the world to break down the barrier, to remove the enmity and to reestablish peace and harmony between man and God. How did he do it? Certainly the Incarnation and all the acts of Jesus' life are part and parcel of our redemption, but it was specifically his sacrificial death out of love for us that accomplished our redemption. As Paul well says in Romans 5:10, "For if while we were enemies we were reconciled to God by the death of his Son, much more, now that we are reconciled, shall we be saved by his life." The same idea appears in Colossians 1:20, "For in him all the fullness of God was pleased to dwell, and through him to reconcile to himself all things, whether on earth or in heaven, making peace by the blood of his cross."

Closely related to the notion of redemption is the idea of "reconciliation." That idea appears in four major Pauline texts in the New Testament. I suggest that you look them up in your Bible: 2 Corinthians 5:18–20; Colossians 1:20–22; Romans 5:10–11; Ephesians 2:11–16. But reconciliation is not just the result of redemption; it was operative during the whole life and death of Jesus, for Paul says that God was in Christ reconciling the world to himself. When we have been finally reconciled with God, we are in a state of peace and harmony with him. The lesson is that God loved man, took the initiative and delivered him from the slavery of sin. He did this by sending his beloved Son into the world to die and to atone for the mysterious evil of sin.

St. John expresses this idea beautifully in his Gospel 3:16–17, "For God so loved the world that he gave his only Son, that whoever believes in him should not perish but have eternal life. For God sent the Son into the world, not to condemn the world, but that the world might be saved through him."

Jesus died for all men

Closely related to the redemption of the human race by the sacrificial death of Jesus is another truth of the Catholic faith, namely, that by his suffering and death Jesus rendered *vicarious atonement* to God for the sins of all mankind. In Catholic theology, "atonement" means reparation for any wrong or injury, either material (such as the loss of something valuable) or spiritual (which is an offense against the honor or dignity of another person).

Material harm requires restitution; moral injury calls for satisfaction or atonement, which is compensation for some wrong done to another person. The word "vicarious" means "in the place of another." Thus, we commonly refer to our Holy Father in Rome as "the Vicar of Christ"; this means that, as the successor of St. Peter as the Bishop of Rome, he takes the place of Christ as the visible head of the Church while the Lord Jesus remains the invisible Head.

We have considered the sin of Adam and the disastrous consequences it had for the human race. Also, because of our weakened human nature and the influence of concupiscence, we all imitate Adam by committing personal sins. Sin, as you will recall, is an offense against God. For such an offense or injury there must be satisfaction or atonement in order to restore the original state of peace and harmony between God and man. The English word "at-one-ment" clearly expresses the revealed truth that the death of Jesus restores the oneness, concord, reconciliation between God and man. Man by himself was not able to effect adequate atonement for his sins because the guilt of sin against God incurs guilt greater than unaided man can atone for. Sin or an offense against God takes on an aspect of the infinite because of the infinite majesty of God, who is offended. Man, being wholly finite, is incapable of offering infinite satisfaction to God for sin.

It is at this point where the importance of our Redeemer, the God-man Jesus Christ, stands out. Fully human and fully divine, Jesus is able to offer himself to the Father in an oblation of love that is acceptable. Being human he can suffer and die; being divine he can offer a sacrifice of love that has infinite value.

It should be noted that Jesus' atonement was *vicarious*, that is, he offered it to God for us, on our behalf, and not for himself. Thus, The Council of Ephesus (431 A.D.) teaches with St. Cyril of Alexandria: "If anyone says that he [Christ] presented His offering for Himself as well and not solely on our behalf [for as He was sinless, He had no need of any offering]: let him be anathema."[3] And the Council of Trent said in 1547: "Our Lord Jesus Christ . . . when we were enemies [see Rom. 5:10], by reason of his very great love wherewith he has loved us [see Eph. 2:4], *merited justification for us* by his own most holy Passion on the wood of the cross, and made satisfaction *for us* to God the Father."[4]

There are many passages in the New Testament that refer to the same truth. Thus, Jesus says in Matthew 20:28, "The Son of man came not to be served but to serve, and to give his life as a ransom for many." St. John's Gospel expresses the same idea in 10:15, "I lay down my life for my sheep." Also, in the Gospel passages that recount the institution of the Holy Eucharist Jesus speaks about "pouring out" his blood for us, and "giving" or "handing over" his body for us. In their own way these passages express the truth taught by the Church that Jesus offered vicarious atonement to God for the sins of man.

The basic reason for the sufficiency of Jesus' atonement lies in the Hypostatic Union. Because of the Hypostatic Union Jesus' every action possesses an intrin-

---

3   DS 261; TCF 606/10.
4   DS 1529; TCF 1932.

sic infinite value because the operating subject is the Second Person of the Blessed Trinity. In fact, not only is Jesus' atonement sufficient for all the sins of the human race, it is superabundant. The reason for this is that every action of Jesus has infinite value. In the fourteenth century Pope Clement VI said that, because of the Hypostatic Union, one single drop of blood of Jesus would have sufficed for the redemption of the whole human race. The pope was merely echoing what St. Paul had taught centuries before: "Where sin increased, grace abounded all the more" (Rom. 5:20).

A final point to consider is that Jesus died for all men, not just for those who are saved. In 1653 Pope Innocent X condemned as heretical the proposition that Christ died for the salvation of the predestined only.[5] And the Council of Trent taught: "God sent him forth as a propitiation by his blood through faith for our sins, not for our sins only, *but also for those of the whole world*" (see 1 John 2:2).[6]

We should not forget, however, that even though salvation is available to all, each one must freely accept it by faith in Jesus Christ and by keeping his commandments.

Jesus merited grace for us

Most of us use the word "merit," at least on occasion, and we all have a general idea of its meaning. Few perhaps would be able to define it or to explain it in any detail. In the Catholic tradition one often encounters expressions

5   DS 1096; TCF 1989/5.
6   DS 1522; TCF 1926.

such as "meriting grace," "meriting eternal life," or "offering up one's merits for the poor souls in purgatory." In fact, the teaching authority of the Church uses the word "merit" to describe how Jesus won grace and eternal redemption for us. The Council of Trent said that Jesus is the "meritorious cause" of our sanctification and justification because he "merited justification for us by his own most holy Passion on the wood of the cross, and made satisfaction for us to God the Father."[7]

We might ask ourselves: What does it mean to "merit" something? In Catholic theology the idea of "merit" means a work performed for the benefit of another, on whom it establishes a claim to give a reward. The idea is closely related to the notion of paying a just price for goods and services rendered. It is also connected with the right to a just wage for work done. If a woman works in a shop for eight hours and the boss has agreed to pay her $15.00 per hour, then at the end of the day she has a right to $120.00. We say that she deserves that amount because she earned it. Thus, we can say that "merit" has something to do with justice and equity. We all know that if someone has done a great favor for us, we are under a certain social obligation to reciprocate the favor in the future if we can or if we are asked.

So merit is the right that one has to a reward. If it is a strict right, Catholic theology calls it *de condigno* merit (the English word for this is "condign," which means "deserved"). If it is a question simply of appropriateness, it is called *de congruo* merit (the English word for this is "congruous" or "suitable").

What has all this got to do with our Lord and Savior

7   DS 1529; TCF 1932.

Jesus Christ, you might be tempted to ask? Well, it has a great deal to do with him if we want to understand how a sinful human being can escape the power of sin and attain eternal happiness with God in heaven. For Jesus' work of redemption is both *satisfactory* (he atoned for our sins) and *meritorious*. The reason is that it both removes the relationship of guilt between humanity and God, and establishes a claim for reward on the part of God.

The Council of Trent defined that original sin is removed only by the merits of Jesus Christ, and that through the Sacrament of Baptism the merits of Jesus are applied to adults and children. Even though the New Testament does not use the word "merit" with regard to Jesus, it does clearly teach the doctrine of his merits. Thus, in Philippians 2:8–9 we read, "He became obedient unto death, even death on a cross. Therefore God has highly exalted him." The glorification and exaltation of Jesus is the reward for his obedience in suffering for our sake. The same idea is presented in Luke 24:26, "Was it not necessary that the Christ should suffer these things and enter into his glory?" (See also John 17:4 and Rev. 5:12.)

We see therefore from the Bible that Jesus, by reason of his obedience and humility, merited for himself his own glorification at the right hand of the Father, that is, resurrection from the dead, Transfiguration of the body, and Ascension into heaven.

All of Jesus' acts, from the first moment of his conception, were meritorious. For they were free, morally good, supernatural, and performed in the state of grace. Since every act of Jesus was the act of a divine Person, each one possessed an infinite meritorious value. In confirmation of this we might note that in 1343 Pope Clement VI taught that "the merits of Christ are infinite."[8]

One consequence of this doctrine is that Jesus merited all supernatural graces received by fallen human beings. All grace of God, therefore, is the grace of Christ. St. Peter testified before the Jewish leaders in Jerusalem: "There is salvation in no one else, for there is no other name under heaven given among men by which we must be saved" (Acts 4:12). And the Council of Trent taught: "No one can be just unless he is granted a share in the merits of the Passion of our Lord Jesus Christ."[9] And St. Paul says in Romans 3:24, "They are justified by his grace as a gift, through the redemption which is in Christ Jesus."

What about our own good acts? Can they be the basis of merit? The answer is, "Yes, they can." But since grace is a completely free gift of God, we cannot merit our initial sanctification *de condigno* (i.e., we don't deserve it). St. Thomas Aquinas says that, once we possess the grace of God, we can merit eternal life *de condigno,* but we cannot merit it for others. We can, however, merit grace for others *de congruo* (i.e., with a well-founded expectation that God will grant it). That is why it is important to pray for the conversion of sinners. And we all sense that the prayers of the saints are very efficacious.

Jesus' descent into the underworld

All Catholics know, or at least should know, the Apostles' Creed, which is said at the beginning of the Rosary. Have

8   DS 1027; TCF 1683.
9   DS 1530; TCF 1933.

you ever wondered why the expression, "He descended into hell," is in the Creed? What does it mean? And what is Jesus, our God and sinless Savior, doing down in *hell*? The statement puzzled me for a long time, and I suspect many Catholics are also puzzled by it. Now I will try to set forth briefly the faith of the Church on this point.

First of all, it should be noted that the English word "hell" is somewhat ambiguous in this particular expression. It corresponds to the Hebrew word "Sheol," the Greek "Hades," and the Latin "Inferus" or "Infernus," and therefore simply means the abode of souls after death without the further notion of punishment. In current English, by the word "hell" we mean the place and state of eternal damnation for the devils and for those who have died in the state of mortal sin as enemies of God. So in the Apostles' Creed the word "hell" means the underworld, the dwelling place of the souls of the dead. It does not mean the hell of damnation. Once this point is grasped it is easier to understand why the Church says that Jesus "descended into hell." The Latin here is clear since it states that Jesus "descendit ad inferos," that is, to the underworld.

The Apostles' Creed expresses the Catholic belief that after his death Jesus' human soul, separated from his body but still united to his divine Person, passed into the abode of the dead. His soul stayed there as long as his body, which also remained united to his divine Person, lay in the tomb, that is, until the morning of his glorious Resurrection.

The New Testament affirms in a number of texts that Jesus "was raised from the dead" (Acts 3:15; 4:10; 1 Thess. 1:10). The implication is that he sojourned among the dead in the underworld (or "hell") from the time of his death until his Resurrection. Jesus himself alluded to this truth when he said: "For as Jonah was three days and three nights in the belly of the whale, so will the Son of man be three days and three nights in the heart of the earth" (Matt. 12:40). In that context "heart of the earth" means the underworld or Sheol.

Speaking of Jesus' Resurrection, St. Peter says, "God raised him up, having loosed the pangs of death, for it was not possible for him to be held by it" (Acts 2:24). Liberation from the "pangs of death" is a symbol of the freeing of the dead from the underworld. Likewise, St. Paul says that Jesus is "the first-born from the dead" (Col. 1:18; see also Rom. 10:6ff.). These texts all point to the fact of Jesus' descent into the underworld after his death.

Some of the early Fathers, such as St. Ignatius of Antioch, St. Justin Martyr, and St. Irenaeus, speak of Jesus being "really raised from the dead." After the fourth century most of the Fathers both of East and West mention the descent of Christ into hell. The belief began to appear in the various Creeds of the Church in the fifth century. It was about that time that the Apostles' Creed as we now have it was codified and handed down to us.

The fact of Jesus' descent into hell is certainly an article of faith, but there is some dispute about his activity there between his death and Resurrection. The explanation of that activity given by St. Thomas Aquinas and the *Catechism of the Council of Trent* is followed by most theologians today. By his death and Resurrection Christ triumphed not only over death, but also over sin and Satan. His sacrificial death therefore reversed the sad consequences of sin. Jesus opened the gates of heaven and made the Beatific Vision a possibility for those who die in faith and charity. So the purpose of his descent into hell was the freeing of the just in limbo by the application of the fruits of the redemption, that is, by the communication of the Beatific Vision.

Jesus did not descend into hell in order to suffer there, or to convert unbelievers or those lacking charity. Thus, his descent brought no deliverance to those who are in hell for their sins and lack of faith. It would seem also that the souls in limbo of children who never had the use of reason while on earth and died in the state of original sin, lacking faith and charity, were not delivered. Recently some Catholic theologians have raised doubts about the existence of limbo, but it has been taught in Catholic schools for a long time. It is still a safe opinion to hold since it has not been rejected officially by the Magisterium of the Church. To the poor souls in purgatory, however, who died with faith and charity, he gave the hope of attaining the Beatific Vision when they had paid their debt of temporal punishment because of their sins and imperfections.

The limbo of the Patriarchs contained the souls of all the saints of the Old Testament, that is, those who died in faith and charity and had paid their debt of temporal punishment. To these Jesus imparted the fruits of grace of his passion. He bestowed on them the Beatific Vision – the vision of God in his essence. Jesus enlightened them right there in the underworld with the Light of Glory. He took all of them with him when he ascended into heaven. Christ descended into all these sections of the underworld by his own power. His very soul, united to his divine Person, descended into the limbo of the Patriarchs and remained there until his Resurrection on Easter morning.

Jesus' Resurrection

There are several unique characteristics of the Catholic faith that distinguish it from all other religions. One of the most important is the Catholic belief in Jesus' Resurrection from the dead. Belief in the Resurrection of Jesus Christ is expressed in all the creeds and rules of faith of the ancient Catholic Church.

In the *Apostles' Creed* we pray: "On the third day he arose again from the dead." Each Sunday at Mass we profess our faith in the Resurrection when we pray the *Nicene Creed* together: He "rose again on the third day in accordance of the Scriptures."

The word "resurrection" means the return of a dead man to life. In the course of history many miraculous resurrections have been produced by the power of God working outside the laws of nature. Jesus, for example, raised from the dead by his own power the young daughter of Jairus (Mark 5:21–42), the only son of the widow of Naim (Luke 7:11–17), and his personal friend, Lazarus, the brother of Martha and Mary (John 11). It is recounted of St. Peter in the Acts of the Apostles that he raised the pious woman Tabitha from the dead (9:36–42). Many other cases could be cited from the Bible and from the lives of the saints.

The resurrection of these persons, however, was very different from that of Jesus. Lazarus and the others were returned from the dead to ordinary, mortal, human life. Eventually they died a second time and permanently; their souls were separated from their bodies and their bodies corrupted in the grave just as all other bodies do.

The Resurrection of Jesus Christ from the dead is something totally different; both his soul and his body take on a whole new mode of existence. His soul was reunited with his body on Easter morning, but this was accomplished *by his own power* and not by the intercession of some other person. The teaching of the Catholic Church emphasizes the fact that Jesus rose from the dead by his own divine power.[10]

Moreover, Jesus' human nature, body and soul, was *glorified* in his Resurrection. It is difficult for us to grasp completely what is meant by the word "glorified." Some of the qualities of glorified humanity of Jesus are mentioned in the Gospels: he is no longer subject to suffering and death; his body possesses a certain radiance that flows from the supreme blessedness of his soul; he can move rapidly from one place to another merely by willing to be there; he has no need of food or sleep; he can pass through other bodies effortlessly – this is indicated by his appearances to the Apostles in the upper room when the evangelist says that the doors were bolted when he entered and appeared to them (John 20:19). The same mysterious phenomenon is alluded to at the conclusion of the story of his appearance to the two disciples on the road to Emmaus. St. Luke writes in 24:31, "Their eyes were opened and they recognized him; and he vanished out of their sight."

Beginning with Jesus' enemies in Jerusalem, there have always been those, both Christian and non-Christian, who have denied the historical reality of his Resurrection. There are many theologians and scripture scholars today who deny the bodily resurrection of the Lord. They attempt to "spiritualize" the meaning of this revealed truth and say that archeologists may some day

10   See DS 539; TCF 634.

find the "bones" of Jesus in a tomb in Jerusalem. That is not what the Catholic Church holds.

In 1907 Pope St. Pius X condemned the following error of the Modernists, many of whom are still among us today: "The Resurrection of the Savior is not properly a fact of this historical order, but only a fact of the supernatural order that is not and cannot be demonstrated; Christian consciousness derived it gradually from other data."[11]

Jesus clearly prophesied that he would rise from the dead on the third day after his death (see Matt. 12:40; Mark 8:31; Luke 9:22; John 2:19). The reality of the Resurrection is proved by the empty tomb and of Jesus' many appearances to his followers during which he spoke with them, ate with them, and allowed them to touch him.

The fact of Jesus' bodily Resurrection from the dead was the central point of the preaching and teaching of the Apostles. The Apostles are primarily "witnesses" of the Resurrection. This point is stressed in many passages in the Acts of the Apostles (see chapters 1, 2, 3, 5, 10, 13). One of the principal qualifications required in the replacement for Judas among the twelve was one who "must become with us a witness to his resurrection" (Acts 1:22).

For Jesus himself, the Resurrection meant his final and definitive entry into the state of glory which was the reward for his humility and obedience in suffering. The Resurrection belongs to the completeness of our redemption. The New Testament associates it with his death on the Cross as one complete whole.

Jesus' Resurrection is the model of our spiritual res-

11   DS 3436; TCF 650/36.

urrection from sin through faith and Baptism (Rom. 6:3ff.) and the pledge or assurance of the resurrection of our own bodies at the Second coming of Christ (1 Cor. 15:20ff.). It is the greatest of all Jesus' miracles; it is convincing proof of his divinity and the strongest proof of the truth of his teaching (1 Cor. 15).

The Ascension of Jesus into heaven

The liturgical feast of the Ascension is celebrated each year on the fortieth day after Easter Sunday. Thus, it always falls on a Thursday, usually in the month of May; in the United States it is a Holy Day of obligation. In some dioceses the feast is transferred to the following Sunday.

The Ascension of Jesus means the transfer of his risen, glorious humanity – body and soul – to heaven, that is, to the spiritual world of God and his angels and saints. St. Luke tells us that he continued to appear to the Apostles for forty days after his Resurrection and spoke to them "of the kingdom of God" (Acts 1:3). At the end of this period he took them to the Mount of Olives, about one mile east of Jerusalem and close to Bethany. While blessing them, he ascended into heaven and disappeared from their sight (Luke 24:50–53).

The Ascension marks the definitive conclusion of Jesus' earthly life. From that moment on he no longer associated intimately, on the physical level, with his disciples. Now the disciples must live in faith, hope, and charity. Jesus is the invisible Head of the Church, gloriously reigning at the right hand of the Father. He will come again at the end of the world to judge the living and the dead.

All the Creeds of the Church affirm belief in Jesus' Ascension. We profess in the Nicene Creed: "He ascended into heaven and is seated at the right hand of the Father."

Jesus ascended into heaven by his own divine power on two counts. In the first place, as the Second Person of the Blessed Trinity he possesses the divine power necessary to transfer his human nature from this material world of time and space to the divine world. In the second place, his transfigured soul has the spiritual power to move his transfigured body wherever and however he wills.

There is no doubt that the place called "the heavens" in Scripture is where Jesus is, while he waits for the Parousia (second coming), remains a mystery to us. We know that this is where God reigns in all his glory, the same place where the angels are said to stand in his presence. St. Mark says that Jesus did not just enter into the heavens, but that he sits at the right hand of God, illustrating that he is now, in all his being, as the Son made man, a partner in the divine rule over the universe.

The biblical expression "to sit at the right hand of God" alludes to Psalm 110:1; the phrase is often used in the Letters of the Apostles, for example, Romans 8:34; Ephesians 1:20; Hebrews 1:3; 1 Peter 3:22. The expression means that the glorified Christ, elevated in his humanity above all the angels and saints, participates in the glory and power of God in a very special way.

Since belief in the Ascension of Jesus is an integral part of the Creed of the Church, it follows that it is a dogmatic teaching of the Church. This great truth is solidly anchored in Holy Scripture, in the tradition of the Church, in the teachings of the Fathers, and in the liturgy.

From the point of view of the salvation of mankind, the Ascension is the ultimate accomplishment of Christ's redemptive work. According to the common teaching of the Church, the souls of the just of the pre-Christian era accompanied the Savior into the glory of heaven: "When he ascended on high he led a host of captives, and he gave gifts to men" (Eph. 4:8).

Jesus ascended into heaven as our forerunner – to prepare a place for us (John 14:2ff.). He also involves us with himself to such a point that St. Paul says that God has "raised us up with him, and made us sit with him in the heavenly places" (Eph. 2:6).

In heaven Jesus also intercedes for his followers: "He is able for all time to save those who draw near to God through him, since he always lives to make intercession for them" (Heb. 7:25). From heaven he sends his gifts of grace, especially the Holy Spirit, into the hearts of the faithful (John 16:7): "It is to your advantage that I go away, for if I do not go away, the counselor will not come to you; but if I go, I will send him to you."

The pouring out of the Spirit on the Church by the glorified Lord is the fruit of his Ascension. One might also call it the first fruit of our perfect association with the Father, who sent him to us from the height of heaven.

The Ascension of Jesus into heaven is the model and pledge of our own ascension and glorification. This was the goal of his voluntary humiliation in the redemptive Incarnation. In a certain sense we might even say that he took us with him when he ascended into heaven, for St. Paul says: "For you have died, and your life is hid with Christ in God. When Christ who is our life appears, then you also will appear with him in glory" (Col. 3:3–4).

BIBLIOGRAPHY

Aquinas, St. Thomas, *Summa Theologiae*, Volumes IV (Christian Classics, Westminster, Md. 1981).

Baker, Kenneth, S.J., *Fundamentals of Catholicism*. Three Volumes (Ignatius Press, San Francisco, Cal. 1982).

_____, *Inside the Bible. An Introduction to Each Book of the Bible* (Ignatius Press, San Francisco, Cal. 1998).

Catechism of the Catholic Church (St. Paul's / Libreria Editrice Vaticana 1994).

Catechism of the Council of Trent (Roman Catholic Books, Fort Collins, Colo. 1923 reprint).

Denzinger-Schönmetzer, *Enchiridion Symbolorum* (Herder, Freiburg in Breisgau 1965).

Hardon, John A., S.J., *Modern Catholic Dictionary* (Doubleday, New York 1980).

Kreeft, Peter, *Catholic Christianity* (Ignatius Press, San Francisco, Cal. 2000).

Neuner, J., S.J., and Dupuis, J., S.J., *The Christian Faith* [Sixth Revised and Enlarged Edition] (Alba House, New York 1996).

Ott, Ludwig, *Fundamentals of Catholic Dogma* (Tan Books and Publishers, Rockford, Ill. 1974).

Solano, Iesu, S.J., *Sacrae Theologiae Summa* III (Biblioteca de Autores Cristianos, Madrid 1956).

The Holy Bible, Revised Standard Version, Catholic Edition (Ignatius Press, San Francisco, Cal. 1994).

Subject Index

Bible Citation Index